the new
sugar & spice

the new
sugar & spice

A RECIPE FOR BOLDER BAKING

Samantha Seneviratne

PHOTOGRAPHY BY ERIN KUNKEL

TEN SPEED PRESS
Berkeley

Library of Congress Cataloging-in-Publication Data
Seneviratne, Samantha.
 The new sugar and spice / Samantha Seneviratne ; photography
by Erin Kunkel. — First edition.
    pages cm
 Includes index.
 1. Pastry. 2. Cookies. 3. Cooking (Spices) I. Title.
 TX773.S384 2015
 641.86'5—dc23

                        2015005473

Hardcover ISBN: 978-1-60774-746-8
eBook ISBN: 978-1-60774-747-5

Printed in China

Design by Ashley Lima

10 9 8 7 6 5 4 3 2 1

First Edition

CONTENTS

for Mohan

INTRODUCTION

About ten years ago, my big brother lived in a sixth-floor walk-up in Little Italy. We were very close, but we didn't talk about how much we loved each other. I don't know many brothers and sisters who do. But I think he knew. And I think the desserts helped.

If I close my eyes, I can still picture him bounding down the stairs to meet me at the front door of his apartment building. He'd run down with a big smile, curly hair tousled, and still in his pajama bottoms after a day spent furiously working on one of his graphic design projects from home. I never felt like climbing his stairs, but I often had deliveries for him. This time, I had made a towering chocolate cream pie the night before and I knew he would want a slice. At least, I knew I wanted to bring him one.

That was our ritual. I would experiment with desserts and Mohan would eat them—whatever the results. When I lived in Brooklyn and he lived in Manhattan, we would make the handoff over dinner at a restaurant near one of our offices. After the tonkatsu or the lasagna had been cleared away, Mohan would sneak bites of my latest triumph—a flaky plum galette, or maybe a custardy bread pudding— surreptitiously from under the table while we talked.

Sometimes, if we didn't have time for a meal, we'd just pick a convenient street corner. We didn't even need to talk much. Meet at Sixth Avenue and West Fourth Street, a kiss on the cheek, a quick transfer of cookie-filled Tupperware, and we'd be on our respective ways.

When I moved to the neighborhood next to his in Manhattan, I could just pop by his apartment anytime and meet him at the bottom of his stairs. My culinary school was just around the corner. On my way home from school, around 11:30 or midnight, I would call him up with a two-minute warning so he could run down to meet me to get something sweet.

After he died, I spent nights awake wondering if he knew how much he mattered to me. I'm sure I hadn't said the words enough. But handing him a big slab of pie or a stack of cookies felt like saying "I love you." I hope he heard me.

Homemade desserts have a big job: they carry important messages to important people. We bake them with the people we love. We share them with the people we love. We eat them with the people we love. But these days, we are told over and over again that one of the principal ingredients of dessert is deadly. The abundance of processed sugar in our diets is a serious health problem. Experts say that sugar is toxic. Some doctors claim that sugar should be grouped with cigarettes and alcohol as a harmful, addictive substance. Sugar has been linked to heart and liver damage, hypertension, and even cancer. Everyone knows that we eat too much of it. According to the American Heart Association, the average American consumes about twenty-two teaspoons of sugar a day. That's about thirteen more teaspoons than their recommended limit. If that's true, then it's no wonder so many of us are left wondering, *Should I bake with my children? Should I give sweets as holiday gifts? What should I serve to the people I love? What should we do about dessert?*

What's even worse is that all this sugar has defeated its own purpose. Too much sugar is causing not only a health crisis but also a deliciousness crisis. Our desserts have become boring, uninspired sugar-bombs, sweetness drowning out everything else that's good. The flood of sugar has diluted real flavor, muffled complexity, and concealed true richness. Too often these days our sweets are *merely* sweet, and sweetness is the only standard a dessert must meet.

My goal in writing this book was to answer the questions that were troubling me: How can we make desserts better? More delicious? Healthier? Better for sharing? How should we bake for the people we love?

How can we make the conclusion of meals more interesting, coffee breaks more exciting, and (dare I say?) life itself more satisfying? The answer was in my cupboard all along: spice!

To get somewhere new, I go back to the past. There was a time when sugar was not ubiquitous and all-powerful, but instead was simply considered one of the spices people used to flavor their foods, satisfy their cravings, and enrich their lives. Before sugar became dominant, the very thought of cinnamon captivated imaginations, governed desires, and made tastes. The flavor and aroma of cloves drove trade, exploration, even war. According to legend, Eden had a scent—cinnamon, ginger, and nutmeg.

And so with *Sugar and Spice,* I wanted to explore a broader spectrum of complementary tastes and flavors, and to reimagine beloved classics as a more balanced blend of sugar and spice. In these recipes, I've tried to take down the sugar to bring up the flavor. I think that less sweet leaves more room for delicious. This book is about making dessert, and the love we share through it, that much more enjoyable and, in turn, a bit better for us, too.

Of course, these are desserts, and sugar is important to baking—not only for flavor but also for texture, color, and aroma. These aren't necessarily low-sugar desserts. But in each recipe, I've used what I believe to be just enough sugar necessary for the best possible experience. In some cases, that isn't very much. In others, it's more. My aim is to make spice an equal partner with sugar, open up a new world of homemade deliciousness, and create new cravings for something other than mass-produced sweetness.

The recipes themselves also tell stories—my own family stories. My parents are from Sri Lanka, the island that some thought held the Garden of Eden itself. I can believe it. Sri Lanka was once one of the most coveted islands on the planet thanks to its fertile land and cinnamon groves—it is the native home of true cinnamon, the species known as *Cinnamomum verum*. But not only cinnamon grows there. When I was growing up, I heard stories about my great-grandmother tending the clove trees that grew thirty feet tall outside her house in the mountains and produced bushels of spice to sell. My grandfather taught my dad how to hand-pollinate their vanilla orchids with a piece of coconut straw pulled from a broom. To me, Sri Lanka was a paradise and a home away from home. I spent some of the most joyful days of my childhood there, helping my grandmother's cook, Tikiri, gather spices from the garden and prepare steaming curries over fire and wood in an open hearth. Back in suburban Connecticut, where I grew up, I ate my fill of chocolate chip cookies, apple pie, and cinnamon buns, along with plenty of cake and brownies from mixes, happily indulging in all the sweet conveniences of my parents' chosen home. But in Sri Lanka, I realized food comes from the earth. There I learned how to eat with my hands and my heart.

The seeds of this book were planted in these distinct places many years ago and grew into an idea while I was working as a magazine food editor, recipe developer, and food stylist in New York City. The result is a tribute to the cozy desserts of my childhood, the American classics that we all know and love, plus a little hint of the exotic in the form of spice.

Now instead of just hankering for a sweet piece of cake, I'm drawn to the spices themselves. On a cold snowy day, something with the bright, spicy heat of ginger might call to me. I know that the smell of cardamom instantly brightens my mood, especially when it's cozied up to chocolate. When I have a heap of fresh summer fruit warming in the sun on my kitchen counter, I reach for cinnamon or vanilla, always crowd-pleasers. The pleasures of sugar and spice together have eclipsed my desire for simply sweet.

The recipes are organized by spice. Some desserts in a designated chapter might use more than one spice, but I've slotted these treats by the flavor that most defines them. If you want the toasty, lemony essence of nutmeg, you know where to turn. And when you're feeling adventurous, flip to the spices that you're less familiar with. Follow your cravings through the book and discover new ones along the way!

I have developed the recipes that follow to bring back to life the power of the spices that once drove global history, and to look for a new way forward. I hope they will make all your traditional favorites feel like new discoveries. And most importantly, I hope you will be excited to share your creations, made with love and sugar and spice, with the people most important to you.

BAKING TIPS, EQUIPMENT, AND INGREDIENTS

These days the wonderful invention we know as the Internet has all the information you will ever need about sourcing ingredients and equipment. But I figured it couldn't hurt to jot down a few tips that will help as you set out to bake the recipes in this book—some thoughts about my favorite tools and ingredients that I would share with you were we baking together. I hope these notes, from one friend to another, will bring you continued success in the sweet kitchen.

GENERAL TIPS

RECIPES Everyone says this. It's the oldest bit of kitchen wisdom in the book. But that's because it's the most important. Make sure you have all the ingredients and equipment handy before you begin. Especially take note of ingredients that are divided between different steps. Adding them all at once when they're supposed to be split up is the easiest mistake to make when you're in the middle of an unfamiliar recipe.

TIME AND TEMPERATURE This is an inconvenient truth about baking, but an important one to know: It's best if you don't rely on time and temperature alone. Every oven is different. And even the same oven can be different on different days. Even if you have an oven thermometer (I have three in mine!), it's best to use sight, smell, and touch along with the clock. The recipes in this book include visual indicators as often as possible to accompany the cooking times. As you bake you will develop baking senses—ways to judge when things are ready to come out of the oven. Use the timer to remind you to stay nearby, and use your baking senses to determine when your masterpieces are ready.

Also, the baking pans you choose can affect baking. A metal pan with a dark finish will bake faster than a metal pan with a light finish and will produce darker edges. Glass baking dishes take longer to heat up, but then retain heat longer than metal pans. My general rule of thumb is to set the timer to alert you at least ten minutes before the first time indicator in a recipe. When you check something early, you give yourself the opportunity to make adjustments before it's too late.

I've found that it takes a little longer to properly preheat an oven than manufacturers would have you believe. My oven takes about thirty minutes to come to temperature. It's helpful to keep an oven thermometer or two in different spots in the oven to know the true temperature at all times.

USING SPICES As you read these recipes, you'll notice that I have a heavy hand when it comes to spices. I just love them! That said, palates are as different as people. While you might like cardamom, you may not like it quite as much as I do.

Or you might like it even more. I've done my best to create recipes with delicious balance, but feel free to experiment. Hold back on the spices you like less and increase the ones you're crazy about. Or follow the recipes as written and see what you think. No matter how you use this book, have fun, eat, and enjoy.

EQUIPMENT

BENCH SCRAPER A bench scraper is a flat, rectangular blade with a handle along one edge. It's great for portioning and trimming dough, lifting and kneading delicate or sticky dough, and cleaning flour-dusted work surfaces and rolling pins. It's also good for cutting butter into flour, absent a pastry blender. Look for a stainless steel scraper with a comfortable handle.

CANDY THERMOMETER A candy thermometer is an inexpensive and useful tool that takes the guesswork out of jobs that are tricky enough as it is, especially boiling sugar and oil. I prefer the metal paddle-type thermometers that sit flat against the side of the saucepan. Let them be your trusted guide for better results in candy making and deep frying.

COOKIE SCOOPS Cookies that are the same size bake up more evenly and beautifully. The easiest way to portion even cookies is to use a cookie scoop. A cookie scoop is simply a small ice cream scoop with a sweeper to knock the dough out of the basin. I find the 1-tablespoon and 2-tablespoon scoops to be the most useful. If you don't have a cookie scoop, measure out one cookie according to the recipe. For example, if the recipe calls for 2-tablespoon scoops, use a measuring spoon to portion out exactly 2 tablespoons of dough. Roll that scoop into a ball and note the size. Use that rolled ball as a visual guide for the rest of the scoops. Cookie scoops are also great for portioning messy cupcake and muffin batters.

ELECTRIC HAND MIXERS AND STAND MIXERS A high-quality hand mixer is an excellent investment. It will cream butter and sugar, mix batter, and whip egg whites and cream like a dream. Practically the only thing it doesn't do well is knead dough, which is a job worth doing by hand. Kneading by hand gives you the opportunity to really learn what bread dough should feel like, when to add flour, and when it's ready to rest. A stand mixer does a quick job of kneading and makes beating up stiff meringues a little easier. If you're lucky enough to have the storage space, both a hand mixer and a stand mixer are worth having. If you've got to choose between them, get the best hand mixer you can find.

MEASURING CUPS AND SCALES Every baker should have two sets of measuring cups in her pantry: one set of dry measuring cups for things like sugar, flour, and cocoa; and 2- and 4-cup glass measuring cups with spouts for liquids. I know it's tempting to use one set for everything, but the two sets are not interchangeable. It's almost impossible to get an accurate measure on something like flour in a liquid measuring cup. In a pinch, you can measure liquid in the dry measuring cups, but it really doesn't work the other way around.

The most accurate way to measure flour without a scale is the "scoop and sweep" method. Start by stirring the flour to aerate it, then use a large spoon to scoop the flour and add it to the measuring cup. Fill the cup up and then use a knife to cleanly swipe the excess away and make it level.

That said, a digital kitchen scale will change your life as a baker. In addition to more accurate results, you'll have fewer dirty bowls and far less mess. Imagine measuring flour by simply tipping it into a bowl on a scale versus the accurate, but somewhat messy, scoop and sweep method. Once you start using a scale, you'll wonder how you ever got on without it.

OFFSET SPATULA My favorite kitchen tool. I have several, in all different sizes. An offset spatula's blade sneaks into tight spaces where regular spatulas can't fit, and it offers more stability than a knife. There is nothing better for icing neatly, or smoothing batters before they go in the oven. It's also helpful for flipping delicate crêpes in a skillet, spreading filling evenly and neatly over dough, or even lifting out a small piece of pie or cake from the pan.

PARCHMENT PAPER Many recipes call for lining a pan with parchment paper. Parchment keeps your goodies from sticking, makes transferring baked goods from the pans easy, and keeps pans clean and tidy. I'll take a quick wash over a deep scrub any day. You can find it in your supermarket near the aluminum foil and plastic wrap.

I buy precut parchment sheets online. They fit nicely on a baking sheet without any measuring or cutting. If you find yourself with a piece of parchment from a roll that won't lie flat in the pan, don't fret. Simply scrunch the paper up into a ball, then spread it out. The sheet will be crinkled but lie nice and flat. To line a baking pan with parchment, start by cutting a piece of paper that is long enough to line the bottom and up two sides of the pan with two inches of overhang. You may have to cut or fold the paper to make it the correct width. Lightly grease the pan with the same fat called for in the recipe. Then press the paper into the greased pan, pressing it into the edges and sides to make a nice tight lining. I like to clip the overhang to each edge of the pan with metal binder clips, one per side, to keep it neat and secure. Then grease the parchment if necessary.

PASTRY BLENDER My favorite tool for cutting fat into flour. Knives will get the job done, but this tool saves time, so the butter stays cold. I prefer the blenders with stiff metal blades as opposed to those with metal wires, because the flexible wires tend to bend and stretch around the cold butter instead of slicing it.

PIE WEIGHTS Essential when a recipe calls for blind-baking an empty pastry crust. The weights keep the dough in place until it is baked and set. Cooking-supply stores sell nice ceramic beads for this job, but plain old dried beans work just as well. Baking beans can be reused for years. Just be sure to label them well. Old baking beans would make terrible soup.

RULERS I know what you're thinking. This seems overly fussy—but I promise that a ruler is a worthwhile investment. A ¼-inch-thick piece of dough will cook longer than an ⅛-inch-thick piece, for example. It's better to know what you've got before the dough goes into the oven. Most importantly, use a ruler to measure your baking pans before you start a recipe. I've seen many a good baker wonder what went wrong after hours of hard work, only to realize that the pan size was wrong. I've done it myself! Buy a ruler.

TIMERS Timers are a busy baker's best friend. It's all too easy to forget about things in the oven, even with the best intentions. My favorite are Polder digital kitchen timers. They are easy to use and have magnets and strings so that you can mount or even wear the timer while you're baking. Wearing your timer may look a little silly, but your cookies will look perfect, which is obviously more important.

INGREDIENTS

BERRIES Washing delicate berries, like raspberries and blackberries, can be tricky. It's best not to wash them until you're ready to use them, as the leftover water can encourage mold. First, line a baking sheet or a plate with a clean dish towel. Fill a bowl with cold water and add the berries. Swish them around gently, then lift them out of the water with your hands and put them on the prepared sheet. This way the dirt stays in the bowl with the water. You can leave them on the towel to dry at room temperature, or, if you're in a hurry, shake the sheet from side to side so that the water shakes off and is absorbed by the towel.

BUTTER All the recipes in this book call for unsalted butter. Different brands of salted butter use different amounts of salt in their blends, so using unsalted butter gives you the ability to control the amount of salt in the recipe. Room temperature butter should be soft enough that you can easily press your finger into it, leaving a clear thumbprint, but not so soft that it is wet and greasy. If your butter has gotten to that point, it's best to start with a new stick and save the soft one for toast. Cut a stick into pieces to speed softening.

CHOCOLATE Unsweetened chocolate is simply roasted ground cacao beans. Bittersweet and semisweet chocolate have added sugar and cocoa butter. Milk chocolate has added milk and even more added sugar. White chocolate is cocoa butter mixed with sugar and milk. The percentages listed on bars of chocolate refer to the percent of cocoa solids and cocoa butter in the blend. In all the recipes in this book I've called for either bittersweet or semisweet. You can use the two interchangeably. Choosing a brand of chocolate for baking is like choosing wine for cooking: if you would enjoy eating it out of hand, then it will be good for baking. Store well-wrapped chocolate in a cool, dry place instead of the refrigerator.

COCOA POWDER Dutch-process (or alkalized) cocoa powder is made from cacao beans that have been washed in a potassium solution. Dutching the beans neutralizes their acidity. Natural (or nonalkalized) cocoa powder, on the other hand, is simply made from ground roasted beans. For the best results, stick to the type noted in the recipe.

COCONUT Virgin coconut oil is fragrant and delicious in baked goods. It's also a great substitute for butter when baking for vegan friends. It is easiest to measure in its liquid state. Just remove the metal lid and pop the jar in the microwave for a few seconds to melt it if necessary and then pour the oil into the measuring cup. These days coconut oil is easy to find in a well-stocked supermarket, health food store, or Asian market. When it comes to coconut meat, I always call for unsweetened shredded coconut instead of sweetened shredded coconut. Although the former is slightly harder to find, I think that the coconut flavor is better and, obviously, it's not cloying.

To toast coconut, spread it in an even layer on a light-colored baking sheet. Bake it at 350°F until golden brown, stirring often, 5 to 10 minutes. Coconut can burn in an instant, so stay close to the oven. You can also toast coconut in a dry skillet, over medium heat, stirring often.

EGG WHITES It's easier to separate cold eggs, but room temperature egg whites whip up higher. Good to know when you're planning to make meringue. Most recipes refer to whipping egg whites to a certain stiffness. How do you know when they've reached the correct peak? It's easy: lift the beaters out of the fluff and see what the peaks do. If they flop over at the tip, the peaks are soft. If they stand straight up and shine, the peaks are stiff.

Take care when beating egg whites without sugar. They are a bit more delicate on their own. When overbeaten, they can separate and become dry and grainy. Beat them to medium-stiff peaks but stop before they look dry.

FLOUR All the recipes in this book were developed and tested using unbleached all-purpose and unbleached bread flour. Except for cake flour, I rarely use bleached flour, which has been chemically treated to create finer, whiter flour. Unbleached flour works well and is easy to find. King Arthur brand is my favorite.

HEAVY CREAM Cold cream whips up faster in a cold bowl. Be sure not to overbeat the cream or else you'll have some fresh butter on your hands (unless of course you'd *like* some fresh butter).

KOSHER SALT It might go against common kitchen wisdom, but I use kosher salt for baking. Some say that the large flakes don't dissolve properly in batters and creams, but I've never had a problem. Diamond Crystal brand kosher salt tastes clean and satisfies all of my salt needs in both sweet and savory cooking. Occasionally I might call for a finishing salt like flaky sea salt. The big, pretty flakes do look nice on top of a batch of caramels. But don't worry. If you don't have any on hand, good old kosher salt will do just fine here, too.

LYLE'S GOLDEN SYRUP If you're not familiar with this stuff, I suggest you head out and buy yourself a can right away. It's wonderful—thick, honey-like syrup made from sugarcane. I often use it instead of corn syrup because I prefer its more interesting, almost toasted sugar flavor. It's also a great substitute for honey when you're baking for the vegans in your life.

NUTS The delicious oils that give nuts their flavor have a tendency to go rancid quickly, so it's best to store nuts in an airtight container in the freezer. The freezer will slow this process. But just in case, give your nuts a taste and make sure they're fresh before adding them to a recipe. Rancid nuts taste sour or bitter and have an unpleasant odor. Trust me. You'll know.

To toast nuts, spread them in an even layer on a baking sheet and bake them at 350°F until lightly browned and fragrant, 8 to 12 minutes, tossing halfway through. Always set a timer. Nuts are one of the easiest things to forget about in the oven.

Unless you've bought blanched nuts, hazelnuts are covered in a thin, papery skin that can add a bitter flavor to desserts. To remove the skin, toast the hazelnuts on a baking sheet until the skins have started to crack and separate from the nut, about 10 minutes. Put the warm nuts on a clean dish towel, wrap them up, and rub them around vigorously. They will rub up against each other and peel themselves. If too many nuts are still covered, pop them back in the oven for another, shorter toast. You don't need to remove all of the skin. Getting about 75 percent of the nuts clean is enough.

ROSE WATER Like tapioca and anise, rose water is another one of those great culinary dividers. People either love it or hate it. I live happily in the first group, and use it in my Orange and Honey Baklava (page 124) and my Love Cakes (pages 66 and 68). That said, not all brands of rose water are created equal. I recommend splurging on a good-quality bottle. It will last you years and the flavor is far superior to the cheap stuff. I like Nielsen-Massey for both rose water and vanilla extract. Store it at room temperature and away from direct heat and sunlight.

SANDING AND PEARL SUGAR Sanding sugar looks like granulated sugar with extra-large grains. Pearl sugar has bright white, coarse grains. Both sugars are used to add a decorative sparkle or crunch to baked goods. Unlike granulated sugar, these sugars won't melt or burn in the oven. Look for them in the baking aisle of your supermarket, online, or in craft and baking supplies stores.

YEAST DOUGHS If your dough doesn't want to rise, pop it into the oven with a baking pan full of boiling hot water on the rack below. The gentle heat and steam should wake up the sleepy yeast.

peppercorn & chile

Growing up in Connecticut, my brother and I fought over food well past the age when we were old enough to know better. I think it could have been our addiction to sugar that fueled the fire—when someone guzzled the last sip of Coca-Cola or gobbled the last pudding pop, things got ugly. The worst spats started with brownies.

In our house, brownies came from a box. The distinction between a homemade brownie and a brownie made at home from a packaged mix simply did not exist. The brownies of our childhood took minutes to whip together, emerged from the oven exactly the same every time, and never fell short of chewy and delicious.

Our love for these perfect confections transformed us from loving siblings into dessert-hoarding monsters. The problem was that we both wanted the edges. When all of that sugar set in the corners of the warped baking pan, something magical happened. The crisp yet perfectly chewy edges of a brownie made from a box were proof of Betty Crocker's status as a manufacturing genius, and I would have ripped out my sweet brother's hair to keep them all for myself.

The battles that resulted drove my mother to come up with a solution. As soon as the freshly baked brownies were cool enough to handle, she would cut all of the edges off and divide them equally between two packages with our names on them. That shut us up for a few minutes—until I had scarfed mine down and my brother started taunting me with his bounty.

This was our experience growing up as first-generation American children of generous parents who were grateful for all the conveniences of their new home. Pancake batter from a carton, mashed potatoes from freeze-dried flakes, and brownies from a mix were the new norm. We ate apples in July and strawberries in December because we could. The connection between food and the earth never seemed all that important. But when we made our summer trips back to Sri Lanka, I got to know a completely different world of food.

My grandparents' house sat on top of a lush former tea plantation among curving coconut palms, sturdy teak trees, and fragrant frangipani. Floppy banana trees flanked the driveway, their shiny elephantine leaves hiding bunches of tiny bananas. The avocado trees farther up the hill were always swollen with ripe, heavy fruit that bowed the branches. Usually we would find giant piles of avocados stacked in the corner of the dining room, ripening and waiting for someone to haul to town to sell. And whenever we arrived, we were greeted with little pyramids of tart green olives, picked by one of the boys in the village and left as presents.

Just down the hill from their house, my grandfather built a house for my mom's younger sister and her family. We call her Punchi, which means "little" in Sinhalese. The path down to Punchi's house was treacherous, always slick with mud after the monsoon rains, and populated by spiders the size of my palm and sneaky leeches that I would discover attached to my ankles hours later. One day when we were making our way down, Punchi stopped to show me a vine of pepper growing up a tree. The dangling strings of green berries reminded me of the long beaded earrings my mom wore to fancy parties. I plucked a few berries off the spike and tasted their citrusy bite.

Pepper is native to the Malabar Coast of southwestern India. I have no idea how it made its way to Sri Lanka on the other side of the Indian subcontinent, specifically to the little patch of land between my grandparents' hilltop home and my aunt's house, but it was not lonely for company there. Quite a few spices grew on my family's land. Nutmeg, cinnamon, cloves, ginger, and cardamom flourished all around us, in addition to pepper. It was hard to imagine that these plants, growing wild and undisturbed, were the same substances contained in the neat jars lined up on the supermarket shelves.

Years later, I can see the beauty in both experiences. My American food story, full of packaged mixes and cinnamon buns at the mall, is anything but unique. Classic American treats make us feel at home, comforted, and taken care of. But in Sri Lanka, I learned that the world of food cannot be contained in a box, and I was introduced to the incredible flavors that grow out of the earth, especially spices.

Today, of course, I make my brownies from scratch, but I use cocoa powder instead of melted chocolate, so the texture is both chewy and cakey, just as those beloved supermarket brownies of my childhood were. I add freshly cracked black pepper, a nod to my Aunt Punchi, its smoky, floral notes mingling with the chocolate in a most unexpected and enticing way. Instead of overwhelming the palate, the sugar in the recipe works in harmony with the other flavors, enhancing their complexity while letting them shine on their own terms. A good-old-fashioned boxed brownie may satisfy the immediate craving for something very sweet, but my brownies have traveled around the world and back. They have tasted the berries of the pepper vines bejeweling the path to Punchi's house.

THE LURE OF PEPPERCORNS

During the Middle Ages, Europeans saw pepper as a link to Paradise, thought to be a very real place somewhere in the East. The little green gems actually grew on the Malabar Coast of southwestern India—which does in fact sound like a kind of paradise. In those days, the landscape on the Malabar Coast was primarily lush rainforest dotted with sparkling lakes and waterfalls.

The pepper trade—one of the most lucrative of the spice trades—was already in full swing by the first century AD. Arab and Indian traders took pepper from the Malabar Coast across the Indian Ocean to the Red Sea. They brought the spice through Egypt to the Nile, shipping it from there to the great trading port of Alexandria. In Alexandria, Venetian and Genoan traders took peppercorns to Italy by way of the Mediterranean.

From there, pepper would heat up the cuisine of every part of Europe. Its desirability meant that the first merchants to find a direct sea route from Europe to the pepper coast—cutting out the middlemen along the traditional pepper trail—would achieve enormous profits. As it turned out, the Portuguese did it in 1497. Pepper was more valuable than gold, and its value was more stable, which makes it a bit clearer why Columbus was so determined to find pepper, among other spices.

What he found instead were chile peppers.

CHILE AND THE ANCIENT WORLD

Chile peppers are native to Central and South America and the Caribbean islands. The people of those regions were eating wild chiles as far back as 7000 BC. By 4000 BC, chiles were among the first crops to be domesticated in the Americas. The combination of chile and chocolate also dates to that time, when the Aztecs began to brew their spicy chocolate drink.

When Christopher Columbus landed in the New World, he was hoping to find the more lucrative spices, but instead he found chile peppers. He wrote to his patrons and told them, "There is also plenty of *ají*, which is their pepper, which is more valuable than [black] pepper, and all the people eat nothing else, it being very wholesome."

In fact, chiles weren't more valuable than peppercorns—Columbus was just doing some advertising. Even if he considered chiles something of a consolation prize, he took them back to Spain. Around the same time, the Portuguese also took chiles they found in southern Brazil to the colonies they were establishing in Asia, including ports in Macao in China and Goa in India. And the rest, as they say, is history.

Yes, peppercorns and chile peppers are distinct species—but even if they aren't botanically connected, I like to think of them as *historically* connected. Peppercorns traveled to Europe from Asia. The European desire for more peppercorns spurred exploration to the New World, where the Europeans found chile peppers. The Portuguese brought chile peppers to Asia—and the food everywhere got more interesting.

WHAT IS PEPPERCORN?

Black pepper, or *Piper nigrum,* is a climbing vine native to southwestern India. When the berries are ripe but still green, they are picked, dipped in water to remove the tough outer covering, and dried. It is during the drying process that the berries turn black. If black peppercorns are soaked, the outer layer, or pericarp, melts away in a process called "retting," leaving only the white seed or white pepper. Green peppercorns are unripe peppercorns used with the outer covering left intact. They are most often brined or dried. Pink peppercorns are not actually peppercorns at all, but the dried berries of a schinus bush.

BUYING AND STORING PEPPERCORN

Like so many spices, once peppercorns are ground they immediately begin to lose their distinctive flavor and scent. Always buy whole peppercorns and grind them as needed with a pepper mill or a spice grinder. You can even crush them between two sheets of parchment using the flat side of a heavy frying pan. Store whole peppercorns in a cool, dry place in an airtight container. They should last at least a year.

WHAT IS CHILE?

Chile is the Nahuatl name for *Capsicum annuum*. Chile peppers are native to Central and South America and the Caribbean islands, and belong to the same family as the tomato and eggplant. As they've adapted to different environments, hundreds of chile varieties have evolved from the *Capsicum* species. Some chiles are picked green while others are allowed to ripen on the vines until red. They are eaten both fresh and dried.

Cayenne pepper is simply dried and ground cayenne chile peppers. The heat of ground cayenne can vary, but the color is a good indicator. Although it is somewhat counterintuitive, the less red the powder is, the hotter it will be. The lighter varieties have a higher ratio of pale seeds to red flesh and that's where most of the heat is in a chile pepper. I'm partial to cayenne pepper in my baking. I find that the sharp, bright heat of cayenne complements other sweet flavors well. But feel free to experiment! Chipotle chile powder, for example, has a smoky edge that would be lovely with chocolate. Ancho chile has that distinct roasted chile flavor without as much heat. The possibilities are endless.

BUYING AND STORING CHILES

The heat of a chile pepper can vary greatly, even within the same variety of pepper. Some jalapeños are mild and some are dynamite. To be safe, I like to give a chile a tiny nibble before I use it to see where it rates on the heat index. The seeds and ribs hold most of the heat in a chile pepper, so if you'd like a lighter touch, remove these with a sharp paring knife before using. Wear gloves as an extra precaution when working with chiles or be sure to wash your hands well when you're finished. Ground cayenne should last up to a year in an airtight container.

BLACK PEPPER, DARK CHOCOLATE, AND SOUR CHERRY BREAD

SERVES 8

1/2 cup (1 stick) unsalted butter, at room temperature, plus more for greasing the pan

2 cups (9 ounces) all-purpose flour, plus more for dusting the pan

1 1/2 teaspoons freshly ground black pepper

1 1/2 teaspoons baking powder

1/2 teaspoon baking soda

3/4 teaspoon kosher salt

3/4 cup granulated sugar

2 large eggs, at room temperature

1 teaspoon pure vanilla extract

1/2 cup sour cream, at room temperature

1/4 cup whole milk, at room temperature

3/4 cup (4 ounces) dried whole tart cherries, chopped

2 1/4 ounces semisweet chocolate (50 to 60 percent cacao), chopped (about 1/2 cup)

Sanding sugar, for sprinkling (optional)

I think you'll be surprised when you taste this cake. Dark chocolate and cherries are obviously delicious together, but the black pepper adds a little smoky heat to mingle with the jammy fruit and bitter chocolate chunks. The idea for combining the three came to me after a glass of dark red wine. Try a warm slice with a glass of your favorite.

Preheat the oven to 350°F. Butter and flour a 4 1/2 by 8 1/2-inch loaf pan.

In a medium bowl, whisk together the flour, pepper, baking powder, baking soda, and salt. In a large bowl, with an electric mixer, beat the butter and sugar on medium speed until pale and fluffy, 3 to 4 minutes. Beat in the eggs, one at a time, scraping down the bowl between additions, and the vanilla. Add half of the flour mixture and beat on low speed until just barely combined. Add the sour cream and the milk and beat briefly, then add the remaining flour mixture and beat just until combined. Fold in the cherries and chocolate.

Spoon the batter into the prepared pan and smooth the top. Sprinkle with sanding sugar. Bake until golden brown and a thin skewer inserted into the center comes out with moist crumbs attached, 50 to 60 minutes. Let cool on a rack for 15 minutes, then flip the loaf out of the pan, turn it right side up, and let it cool completely. I prefer eating this bread warm, the day that it's made.

Store leftovers, well wrapped, at room temperature for up to 2 days, or frozen for up to 1 month.

CHILE-CHOCOLATE TRUFFLES

MAKES 64 SMALL TRUFFLES

1 pound bittersweet chocolate (60 to 70 percent cacao), very finely chopped (about 4 cups)

¾ cup heavy cream

2 tablespoons unsalted butter

3 Thai bird chiles, stemmed and minced

¾ teaspoon kosher salt

1 teaspoon pure vanilla extract

Like most people, my mom likes a strong cup of tea with a bite of something sweet. But unlike most people, she also likes it with a taste of something spicy. When I was a kid, I used to watch in awe as she nibbled through a few Thai bird chiles alongside her tea and a piece of chocolate. She used to hold up the chiles and say, "These are dynamite!" before biting into one of the shiny little red and green peppers. Only now do I see the brilliance in her habit. I made these truffles for my mom. Fresh chiles add a refreshing, almost crisp heat to the dark, creamy chocolate. Thai bird chiles can be found in the produce section of any well-stocked supermarket or Asian market. If you can't find Thai bird chiles, jalapeños make a nice substitute. Since there are so few ingredients, the most important thing when making truffles is to start with a chocolate that you love. Bittersweet chocolate has a cacao percentage of around 60 to 70 percent. If you prefer something a little lighter, try semisweet chocolate. I don't recommend milk or white chocolate for this, as they both are more likely to seize up.

Line an 8-inch square baking pan with parchment paper, leaving a 2-inch overhang on two sides.

Set the chocolate in a medium bowl. In a small saucepan, bring the heavy cream, butter, chiles, and salt to a boil over medium heat and then immediately pour it over the chocolate. Cover the bowl with plastic wrap and let stand 2 minutes. Whisk the chocolate mixture until smooth, add the vanilla extract, and pour into the prepared pan. Cover with plastic wrap and chill until firm, at least 2 hours. When the chocolate is firm, cut around the edges to release it from the pan. Using the parchment, transfer the chocolate onto a cutting board. Cut into 64 squares. Store the truffles in an airtight container in the refrigerator for up to a week.

CRUNCHY PEANUTPEPPER COOKIES

MAKES ABOUT 2 DOZEN COOKIES

1¼ cups (5⅝ ounces) all-purpose flour

1¼ teaspoons kosher salt

¾ teaspoon cayenne pepper

½ teaspoon baking soda

½ cup (1 stick) unsalted butter, at room temperature

⅓ cup granulated sugar, plus more for pressing

½ cup packed light brown sugar

½ cup natural, unsweetened peanut butter, stirred well

1 large egg, at room temperature

1 teaspoon pure vanilla extract

¾ cup (3¾ ounces) roasted, salted peanuts, coarsely chopped

I love Hot Mix, the ubiquitous (in South Asian cupboards at least) spicy and salty snack made with a mix of peanuts, raisins, and crunchy noodles. On a recent trip to Kalustyan's, the New York spice and specialty food haven, I noticed that Hot Mix is only one of the dozens of spicy snack mixes they carry. There was a whole wall dedicated to the stuff, which is significant when you think of the cost of Manhattan real estate. It got me thinking. How can I put that flavor into a cookie?

So I came up with these. If you like a classic peanut butter cookie, you'll love this upgraded version. The extra salt and cayenne cover the whole spectrum of cravings. The recipe uses natural peanut butter without added sugar—it has a more delicious, purer peanut flavor. My favorites are Smucker's Natural Peanut Butter and Cream-Nut. Be sure to stir the jar well to distribute the oil evenly before you scoop it into the measuring cup.

Line two baking sheets with parchment paper. Preheat the oven to 350°F. In a medium bowl, whisk the flour, salt, cayenne, and baking soda. In a large bowl, stir the butter, granulated sugar, and brown sugar until creamy. Stir in the peanut butter, egg, and vanilla. Add the flour mixture to the peanut butter mixture and stir to combine. Stir in the peanuts.

Scoop the dough into 2-tablespoon balls and place on the prepared sheets at least 2 inches apart. Using a fork dipped in sugar, gently press a crisscross pattern in the top of each cookie, flattening it out to a 2-inch circle.

Bake until the cookies are light brown around the edges and on the bottom, 12 to 14 minutes, rotating the sheets halfway through. Let the cookies cool for 5 minutes on the sheets on racks, then move them to the racks to cool completely. Store in an airtight container at room temperature for up to 2 days or in the freezer for 1 month.

HOT HONEYCOMB CANDY

MAKES ABOUT 1 POUND CANDY

Butter, for the pan

¾ cup sugar

¼ cup mild honey or Lyle's Golden Syrup

2 teaspoons distilled white vinegar

⅛ to ¼ teaspoon cayenne pepper, depending on how spicy you'd like it

Pinch of kosher salt

2 tablespoons water

2 teaspoons baking soda

1 pound bittersweet chocolate (60 to 70 percent cacao), chopped (about 4 cups)

I've been in the candy business a long time. When my brother and I were small, we used the money he earned on his paper route to buy candy in bulk and sell it to the neighborhood kids. We'd stroll down the street, our green wheelbarrow laden with Nerds and Pop Rocks, singing "Candy for sale!" and the kids would flock to us. Funny little entrepreneurs.

These days, I prefer to make candy rather than to sell it. Honeycomb candy, with its feathery crunch, is one of the simplest to make. The process couldn't be easier, but it moves very quickly. The key is to have all your ingredients and tools lined up and at the ready. Covering the pieces in chocolate is not only tasty, but the chocolate also acts as a barrier to moisture and keeps the candy fresher longer.

Butter an 8-inch square pan and line with aluminum foil with a 1-inch overhang on two sides. Butter the foil and any exposed sides of the pan. Grab a small whisk, a heat-safe spatula, a small plate, and an oven mitt, and set them by the stove.

In a medium saucepan fitted with a candy thermometer, combine the sugar, honey, vinegar, cayenne, salt, and water. The mixture will swell up to about four times the volume in the next step so make sure the pot is big enough. In a small bowl, set aside the baking soda.

Heat the sugar mixture over medium-high heat to 300°F without stirring. In order to get an accurate reading, make sure the bulb of the candy thermometer is submerged in the sugar mixture. You may have to hold the pot tipped to the side while the sugar cooks. Use the oven mitt to protect your hand and arm from steam while you hold the pot. Remove the pot from the heat, quickly remove the thermometer and place it on the plate, and immediately whisk in the baking soda. Take care to disperse the baking

CONTINUED

soda evenly, but don't mix for longer than a second or two or you'll deflate the bubbles. Quickly scrape the mixture into the prepared pan. Don't touch it once it goes in the pan so as not to disturb the bubbles. The mixture will swell up and then deflate. Let it stand until completely cool and hard, about 30 minutes.

Line two baking sheets with parchment paper.

Place the chocolate in a bowl over a pot of barely simmering water, stirring occasionally, until the chocolate is melted. Make sure that the bottom of the bowl is not touching the water. Alternatively, you could melt the chocolate in the microwave, in 15-second bursts, stirring in between each one.

Lift the candy from the pan and pull off the foil. Break the candy into 1- to 2-inch pieces. Transfer the chocolate to a deep, narrow dish, like a 2-cup glass measuring cup. Using a fork to lift the candy, dip each piece into the chocolate and toss it to cover it completely. Pick the coated candy up and tap it on the edge of the dish to knock off any excess chocolate. Set the candy on the prepared baking sheet and repeat with the remaining pieces. Pop the sheets in the fridge for a few minutes to set the chocolate.

Store the candy in an airtight container at room temperature for up to a week (if it's not too hot) or in the fridge for up to a month.

MEXICAN HOT CHOCOLATE POPS

MAKES 10 POPS

1½ cups heavy cream

1½ cups whole milk

4 large egg yolks

3 tablespoons sugar

1 tablespoon Dutch-process cocoa powder

1 teaspoon ground cinnamon

½ teaspoon kosher salt

⅛ to ¼ teaspoon cayenne pepper, depending on how much you like heat

4 ounces semisweet chocolate (50 to 60 percent cacao), chopped (about 1 cup)

Ancient Mesoamericans like the Mayans and Aztecs drank their chocolate piping hot with honey and ground corn. I like mine ice cold with plenty of creamy milk. But we do share one similarity: we both like it a little spicy. The note of heat makes these a treat for pudding pop addicts of all kinds.

Set a fine-mesh sieve over a large liquid measuring cup (for easy pouring). Have ready ten 3-ounce ice pop molds and 10 ice pop sticks.

In a medium saucepan, whisk together the cream, milk, yolks, sugar, cocoa, cinnamon, salt, and cayenne and cook over medium heat, stirring constantly, until just thick enough to coat the back of a spoon, 6 to 8 minutes. If you can draw a clear line that holds through the mixture on the back of a wooden spoon, it's done.

Strain the mixture into the measuring cup, add the chocolate, and let it stand for 5 minutes. Whisk to incorporate the melted chocolate. Fill the molds, cover, add sticks, and freeze until firm, at least 12 hours.

To release the pops, run the bottom of the mold under warm water very briefly. Serve right away or store individually in small, resealable plastic bags for up to 2 weeks.

MANGO LIME SORBET

MAKES ABOUT 1 QUART

4 to 5 large mangoes (9 to 10 ounces each), preferably Champagne

6 tablespoons sugar

6 tablespoons Lyle's Golden Syrup or mild honey

¼ cup water

½ teaspoon finely grated lime zest (from 1 lime)

¼ cup freshly squeezed lime juice (from 2 limes)

⅛ to ¼ teaspoon cayenne pepper, depending on how much you like heat

Chopped pistachios, for serving

My favorite way to eat a spear of fresh mango is standing up in the kitchen, plucked off the tip of my dad's knife. He's the master at removing the skin of the fruit in long, multicolored spirals with a sharp paring knife. When he's finished peeling it, he slices up big, juicy wedges in the palm of his hand and doles them out, speared on his knife. I have many fond memories of standing around in the kitchen, chatting and munching on sweet, ripe mango for dessert.

This sorbet is beautifully simple—the essence of a fresh slice of fruit. Champagne mangoes, also known as Ataulfo mangoes, taste of honey and smell like flowers. I think they make a perfect sorbet. Besides having a complex flavor, they seem to be less fibrous than other varieties. If you can't find Champagne mangoes, just be sure to find the ripest, most fragrant fruit available. Puree the fruit to a very smooth consistency to ensure the silkiest sorbet. If you have any extra puree, add it to your next smoothie or spoon it over pound cake.

Peel each mango and cut the flesh off the pit. Chop the flesh and add to a blender. Puree until very smooth. Reserve 3 cups for the sorbet. Save any extra for another use.

In a small saucepan, combine the sugar, syrup, and water over medium-low heat. Cook, stirring, until the sugar has dissolved, 2 to 4 minutes. Remove from the heat and let cool completely. In a medium bowl, combine the cooled sugar mixture, reserved mango puree, lime zest and juice, and cayenne. Cover with plastic wrap and refrigerate until very cold, at least 2 hours.

Stir the cold mango mixture and then freeze it in an ice cream maker according to the manufacturer's instructions. Spoon into a freezer-proof container and freeze until firm. Top with pistachios to serve.

S'MORE PIE

SERVES 8 TO 10

CRUST

2 cups (about 8 ounces) graham cracker crumbs

6 tablespoons (¾ stick) unsalted butter, melted

2 tablespoons sugar

½ teaspoon kosher salt

FILLING

8 ounces bittersweet chocolate (60 to 70 percent cacao), chopped (about 2 cups)

1 cup heavy cream

2 large eggs, lightly beaten, at room temperature

1 teaspoon pure vanilla extract

½ teaspoon kosher salt

TOPPING

2 egg whites

⅔ cup sugar

¼ cup water

1 teaspoon freshly ground black pepper

½ teaspoon pure vanilla extract

I don't really like camping. Nature is okay with me, but I like to experience it and then take a good, hot shower, cook dinner on a powerful gas range, and sleep in a clean, cozy bed. But I do love a s'more. To me, they are basically the only reason to ever don a heavy backpack.

This pie is a pretty, sliceable riff on s'mores that hits all the right notes: salty-sweet graham crust, luscious bittersweet chocolate custard, and a light, fluffy toasted black pepper meringue. Eat it while watching a movie, soaking in the tub, or doing something else supremely comfortable.

Making the meringue topping is easy, especially if you have a stand mixer. If you only have a hand mixer, enlist the help of a friend to beat the egg whites while you keep an eye on the temperature of the sugar. It's doable alone, but more fun with help.

Preheat the oven to 350°F.

To prepare the crust, combine the graham crackers, butter, sugar, and salt in a 9-inch fluted tart pan with a removable bottom or a standard 9-inch pie plate. Press the crumbs into the bottom and sides of the pan. Bake the crust on a baking sheet until fragrant and just beginning to brown, 14 to 16 minutes. Let the tart shell cool completely on the sheet on a rack.

To prepare the filling, put the chocolate in a medium bowl. In a small saucepan, bring the cream just to a boil over medium heat. Pour the hot cream over the chocolate and let stand for 1 minute. Whisk until smooth and let cool slightly. Stir in the eggs, vanilla, and salt. Pour the filling into the prepared crust. Set the pie on a baking sheet and bake until the edges of the filling are set but the center still has a slight jiggle, 18 to 22 minutes. Let the pie cool completely on a rack.

CONTINUED

Just before serving, make the topping. In a large bowl (or the bowl of a stand mixer fitted with the whisk attachment) add the egg whites. In a small saucepot fitted with a candy thermometer, heat the sugar and the water over medium-high heat without stirring. When the thermometer hits about 220°F, beat the egg whites on medium speed until just frothy and the yellowish hue has disappeared. When the sugar reaches 238°F, increase the mixer speed to high and, with the mixer running, pour the sugar syrup into the bowl in a thin stream. Continue to beat the mixture until shiny, medium-stiff peaks form and the mixture is cool, about 6 minutes. You should be able to lift the beaters out of the mixture and pull tall, stiff peaks that fold over at the tip. Beat in the pepper and vanilla.

Scoop the meringue on top of the pie and use an offset spatula to swirl it around into decorative swoops and spikes. Using a mini blowtorch, toast the topping to an even golden brown. This pie is best the day it's made, served at room temperature.

SWEET FIG AND BLACK PEPPER SCONES

MAKES 8 BIG SCONES

¼ cup cold heavy cream, plus more for brushing

¼ cup cold buttermilk

1 large egg plus 1 large egg yolk

1 teaspoon pure vanilla extract

2¼ cups (10⅛ ounces) all-purpose flour, plus more for the work surface

¼ cup granulated sugar

1 tablespoon baking powder

1½ teaspoons freshly ground black pepper

½ teaspoon kosher salt

½ cup (1 stick) cold unsalted butter, cut into pieces

4½ ounces dried Mission figs, stemmed and finely chopped (about ¾ cup)

Sanding sugar, for sprinkling (optional)

A good scone hits just the right note between sweet and savory. The crumb should be tender and craggy, never too sugary, and serve as the perfect vehicle for plenty of melted butter or clotted cream. These scones come with the added bonus of chewy dried figs and the bite of freshly ground black pepper, both of which complement the aforementioned butter and cream beautifully.

Scones are a breeze to whip up. If they didn't have to chill, they'd take almost no time at all. They are really best the day they're made, preferably just moments out of the oven. In order to achieve that bliss any time, freeze the shaped scones in an airtight container then bake from frozen as needed and desired.

In a small bowl, stir together the cream, buttermilk, egg, egg yolk, and vanilla. In a large bowl, whisk together the flour, sugar, baking powder, pepper, and salt. Using a pastry blender or two knives, cut the butter into the flour mixture until it is the texture of coarse meal with some larger pea-size pieces. Add the figs and toss to combine.

Line a baking sheet with parchment paper.

Add the cream mixture to the flour mixture and mix with a fork just until a shaggy dough forms. Tip the mixture out onto a lightly floured surface and knead it, just 2 or 3 times, to get the mixture to come together. Try not to overwork the dough. Form the dough into a 6-inch circle. Using a sharp knife, cut the dough into 8 equal triangles. Spread the triangles out evenly on the prepared sheet. Freeze for 20 to 30 minutes. Meanwhile, preheat the oven to 400°F.

Brush the tops of the frozen scones with cream and sprinkle with sanding sugar. Bake the scones until golden brown and a toothpick inserted into the center comes out clean, 15 to 18 minutes. Completely frozen scones may take a few extra minutes. These are best eaten warm.

SALT AND PEPPER CARAMEL BROWNIES

MAKES 16 LARGE OR 25 SMALL BROWNIES

BROWNIES

½ cup (1 stick) unsalted butter, melted and slightly cooled, plus more for greasing the pan

¾ cup (3⅜ ounces) all-purpose flour

¾ cup (2¼ ounces) Dutch-process cocoa powder

2½ teaspoons freshly ground black pepper

½ teaspoon baking powder

1 cup packed dark brown sugar

2 teaspoons pure vanilla extract

½ teaspoon kosher salt

2 large eggs

CARAMEL

2 tablespoons water

⅔ cup granulated sugar

⅓ cup heavy cream

2 tablespoons unsalted butter

1 teaspoon pure vanilla extract

1 teaspoon fleur de sel or kosher salt, for sprinkling

They say that freshly ground black pepper wakes up the salivary glands and enhances our ability to taste food. Who wouldn't want to taste their brownies more completely? Black pepper also adds an unexpected smoky, floral note to the classic treat, making them complex and irresistible. The bittersweet, salty caramel is indulgent but heavenly. Whole batches of these have been known to disappear in our house in less than forty-eight hours.

Preheat the oven to 325°F. Butter an 8-inch square baking pan and line it with parchment, leaving a 2-inch overhang on two sides. Butter the parchment.

To prepare the brownies, whisk together the flour, cocoa, pepper, and baking powder in a medium bowl. In a large bowl, whisk together the brown sugar, vanilla, salt, and eggs. Add the melted butter to the sugar mixture and whisk until smooth. Fold in the flour mixture. (You could throw in some chocolate chips at this point, but that might just be gilding the lily.)

Pour into the prepared pan and bake until just set, 24 to 26 minutes. As soon as a toothpick inserted 2 inches from the center pulls out very moist crumbs, not runny batter, pull the brownies out of the oven. Set on a rack to cool.

To prepare the caramel, add the water to a medium saucepan. Add granulated sugar to the center of the saucepan, making sure the sugar is evenly moistened. Cook over medium heat, without stirring (although you can gently swirl the pan, if necessary), until the caramel is medium amber in color, 5 to 6 minutes. Slowly add the cream, whisking constantly; be very careful, since it will bubble up and spatter. Add the butter and cook, whisking constantly, until the caramel is smooth and slightly thickened, 2 to 3 minutes more. Whisk in the vanilla. Pour the caramel over the brownies and spread evenly.

CONTINUED

Cool in the pan, on a rack, for about 10 minutes. Sprinkle with fleur de sel and refrigerate until the caramel is set, about 1 hour.

To serve, cut around the edge of the brownies to loosen them from the pan, then use the parchment to lift the brownies out of the pan and onto a cutting board. Use a long sharp knife to cut the brownies into squares. (Little pieces go a long way!) Store the brownies in an airtight container at room temperature for up to 3 days.

cinnamon

When I was little, I spent every minute I could outdoors. My brother and I were always tromping around in the woods around our neighborhood, building tents and forts. But whenever we traveled to visit my grandparents in Sri Lanka, I planted myself inside, in the kitchen, where the housework was going on— something I never would have done at home.

The kitchen of my grandparents' mountain bungalow in Sri Lanka was simple. It had a concrete floor, a lightbulb that swung down from exposed wires, and a fire in an open hearth. Old glass jars that had once been full of coffee and Milo, the tasty malt powder beloved by kids around the world, were reborn as a makeshift pantry and filled with turmeric, homemade curry powders, a block of rock salt in water, and coconut oil. Speedy geckos scampered along the paint-chipped walls and sleepy stray dogs lounged on the front steps. Compared to our gleaming kitchen at home in Connecticut, it felt rustic, strange, and cozy. Clean—but still the kind of place where a spill wasn't the end of the world.

I spent so much time in that kitchen that eventually my grandmother set up a spot designated specifically for me. Parked along the wall next to the hearth was a blue wooden bench where I would sit for hours watching Tikiri, my grandmother's cook. I remember her as being forever twenty, with lustrous hair, a big, warm smile, and the same three polyester flower-print dresses, always worn in rotation. Tikiri didn't speak much English, and the only Sinhalese phrase I knew was "I'm hungry," but communication never posed a problem. For the most part, I was a humble and silent spectator, but when it came to squeezing dough through a hand press to make the rice noodle nests called string hoppers, or grinding the meat out of coconut halves, I was thrilled to be enlisted to help.

I was nine years old when Tikiri and my grandmother finally let me cook something of my own—a traditional Sri Lankan dessert called love cake, a fragrant, dense blondie-like confection. I remember everything we did that afternoon. Tikiri set up the fire and laid the ingredients out in order on a banana leaf, nature's disposable plate, and I took it from there. There was pearly semolina, different from the regular flour I was expecting and all the more special; cashews and candied fruit chopped into perfect cubes; and my grandmother leaning over my shoulder to help me add each ingredient at just the right time. The potent smell of honey, rose water, cinnamon, and cardamom mingled in the air and lingered on the spoons we used, which were made of coconut shells. When it was ready, we cut the golden cake into neat diamonds and served it with tea: it was crunchy and chewy on the outside, soft and creamy-sweet on the inside, and studded with the fruits and nuts we had carefully measured.

Looking back, I can see that the love cake I made in my grandmother's cozy kitchen tells a story much larger than my family's story. The recipe I made that day had been in the making for centuries. Historians believe that the Portuguese brought the European-style cake-making tradition to Sri Lanka in the fifteenth century. Fragrant rose water, considered an integral part of traditional love cake, is a distinctively Arabian contribution and was probably brought to Sri Lanka even earlier than that. Over the centuries, the Sri Lankans made the recipe their own by adding local ingredients—cashews, cinnamon, and cardamom.

But the question behind this cosmopolitan cake is, why did the Arabs and Portuguese end up in Sri Lanka in the first place? They came for the cinnamon.

THE CINNAMON ROUTE

True cinnamon (*Cinnamomum verum* or *Cinnamomum zeylanicum*) is native only to Sri Lanka. Arab traders first brought cinnamon from Sri Lanka into the wider world as many as four thousand years ago. For millennia, the great "Cinnamon Route" linked the Indian Ocean to the Arab world, Africa, and the West beyond. To protect their monopoly and maximize the value of their product, the traders perpetuated fantastic myths that obscured cinnamon's origin and scared off the competition. Their stories were taken very seriously. Theophrastus, a Greek student of Aristotle (now known as the father of botany), wrote that cinnamon grew in Arabia on bushes in ravines guarded by poisonous snakes. He described how the cinnamon was divided after it was gathered, leaving one-third of the harvest as an offering to the sun god, who would then protect the harvesters against the poisonous snakes on subsequent visits. These stories helped to keep the Arab traders on top for thousands of years.

But by the fifteenth century, Europeans, finally wise to the Arabian stories, were trying desperately to wrest the lucrative spice trade from Arab control by uncovering a sea route to Asia. Christopher Columbus thought he could get there by sailing directly west, and he appealed to the Portuguese for funding. The Portuguese weren't buying it, but Ferdinand and Isabella of Spain took the bait. They had high hopes for Christopher Columbus's quest for a faster route to the spice paradise of the East Indies.

Spices were so important to his voyage that even after making landfall in the New World, exploring, and claiming for Spain an unknown, unmapped hemisphere, he was under immense pressure to deliver the goods. In a letter back to his patrons, Columbus tried to assure them that their investment was not lost. He wrote, "In Española there are many sources of spices, as well as large mines of gold and other metals. I believe I have found rhubarb and cinnamon." We know that cinnamon did not grow in the Americas, but it's not clear that Columbus lied outright. Perhaps he had simply convinced himself that the plants he found were cinnamon because he wanted to believe it. But it is clear what he and his employers thought important. A "new world" was one thing, but cinnamon was the real prize.

Unfortunately for the Spanish, the Portuguese did figure out how to get to the East and to the precious cinnamon by sailing around the southern cape of Africa. They set up pepper ports in India and then made their way to Sri Lanka. They arrived in Cilao, as they called it, in 1505, bringing guns and armor along with their cake recipes. The king of the lowland Sinhalese, who ruled the coast, welcomed them and offered cinnamon in exchange for protection from his enemies—the highland King of Kandy, the Northern Tamils, and Muslim traders. It was only a matter of time before the Portuguese pushed the king aside and took control of the spice trade. A year after their arrival, over eleven tons of cinnamon made its way to Lisbon.

The highland Kingdom of Kandy—protected by the same mountains that surround my grandmother's house—survived Portuguese rule intact, but eventually made its own tactical miscalculation. In the early seventeenth century, the king made a deal with the Dutch to rid his domain of the Portuguese. The Dutch East India Company forced the Portuguese out between 1636 and 1658. Then they subverted the king's authority and renamed their valuable spice island Zeylan. They controlled the world trade in cinnamon until 1796, when the British East India Company ousted them and claimed the island—renamed Ceylon—for themselves. They controlled it until 1948, the year of Sri Lankan independence.

These days, Ceylon cinnamon continues to grow mostly in Sri Lanka, while cassia is grown in Indonesia, China, and Vietnam. Early in the twentieth century, American traders began to import cassia due to the rising price of Ceylon cinnamon. Now cassia is much more common in the United States.

WHAT IS CINNAMON?

There are dozens of plants that fall under the *Cinnamomum* genus, but the two most common are true cinnamon, sometimes called Ceylon cinnamon, and Chinese cinnamon, or cassia.

Ceylon cinnamon is lighter, with notes of honey, vanilla, and citrus. Cassia is more robust with a spicier kick. In the United States, the spice most often labeled simply as "cinnamon" is in fact cassia, but both types are worth seeking out.

I prefer to use Ceylon cinnamon for more delicate applications. When the spice isn't competing with a lot of other flavors, its subtle complexity can shine through. It's perfect for sprinkling on oatmeal or toast, or in recipes like my Cinnamon, Hazelnut, and Date Buns (page 56) or Blueberry Custard Tarts (page 53). Cassia's bright heat shines in tandem with other spices, creamy frostings, and rich batters. Cassia is perfect in recipes like the Parsnip Cake with Cream Cheese Frosting (page 187), where it complements and enhances the ginger.

Both cassia and Ceylon cinnamon come from evergreen trees in the laurel family. In order to harvest the spice, the outer bark of the tree must be stripped away. The inner bark is peeled off in sheets and scraped clean. The sheets are then trimmed and dried—as they dry, they roll up into quills. The quills are then cut into segments or ground into powder for sale. The bark is harvested after rainy seasons, when the damp bark is easier to collect.

BUYING AND STORING

In the United States, the spice labeled simply as cinnamon is most often cassia. Ceylon cinnamon is a bit less common and usually labeled specifically as such. Visually, they are fairly easy to tell apart. Ground cassia is slightly darker in color than Ceylon cinnamon and the quills are much sturdier. Ceylon cinnamon quills are distinctly thin and fragile. Their respective aromas also differ. Ceylon cinnamon smells sweet and round, while cassia has a sharpness to its aroma reminiscent of Red Hots candy. Don't worry if you can only find one or the other. While one may be better suited to certain applications than the other, they can be used interchangeably.

As a more flavorful alternative to using preground cinnamon, buy whole sticks and grate them for each use. Sturdy sticks of cassia are best grated with a common kitchen rasp (the same one you'd use for nutmeg or hard cheese). A spice grinder works well for more delicate Ceylon cinnamon sticks. Cinnamon sticks will last up to two years if the quills are stored properly in an airtight container. Ground cinnamon loses its flavor much faster and should be replaced every 3 to 6 months.

SUMMER BERRY FOCACCIA

SERVES 12

½ cup (1 stick) butter, melted, plus more for greasing the bowl and the work surface

2 cups (9 ounces) bread flour

2 cups (9 ounces) all-purpose flour

½ cup sugar

2½ teaspoons active dry yeast

1 teaspoon kosher salt

1½ cups warm water (105°F to 110°F)

1 large egg, lightly beaten

12 ounces (about 2½ cups) fresh fruit, such as blueberries, raspberries, small blackberries, or pitted, quartered cherries

¾ teaspoon ground cinnamon

My dad has an indefatigable sweet tooth. Sometimes he doesn't agree with my "less sweet is more delicious" idea. He declared one cake I made (which was plenty sweet, just for the record) "one step away from bread" as he huffed off to look for a chocolate bar. Ah well. You can't win them all. But his comment did give me a great idea.

Who doesn't love the pillowy-soft chew of a perfect olive oil focaccia? The sweet version, popular in some parts of Italy, is even better. I've swapped the olive oil for melted butter, enriched the dough with an egg and a little sugar, and topped it with plenty of cinnamon to complement the perfectly tart, summer berries that melt down and juice out as it bakes. I think Dad would agree that this brunch star is one step *above* bread.

Lightly butter a large bowl and set aside.

In the bowl of a stand mixer fitted with the paddle attachment, or in a large bowl, combine the bread flour, the all-purpose flour, ¼ cup of the sugar, the yeast, and the salt. In a small bowl, combine the water, ¼ cup of the melted butter, and the egg. With the mixer on low, or using a wooden spoon, add the water mixture to the flour mixture and mix until a dough starts to form. If using a mixer, switch to the dough hook and knead the dough until smooth and elastic, about 5 minutes. To knead the dough by hand, use a bench scraper or a large metal spatula in one hand to lift and fold the dough onto itself, and the other hand to knead for about 10 minutes. (Just remember to take off any rings before you get started!) The dough should be very sticky and wet and may not become completely smooth but don't add extra flour.

Using a bench scraper or a rubber spatula, put the dough in the prepared bowl. Form it into a ball, cover lightly with plastic wrap, and leave it in a warm, draft-free spot until

CONTINUED

it has doubled in size. This could take anywhere between 30 minutes and 2 hours. It all depends on how warm your house is.

Tip the doubled dough onto a lightly buttered work surface and knead it a few times to deflate it, then fold it over itself at twelve, three, six, and nine o'clock. Put it back in the bowl, seam side down, cover with plastic wrap, and let it rise again until almost doubled, about 1 hour.

Preheat the oven to 450°F. Spread 2 tablespoons of the remaining melted butter in a 15½ by 10½-inch jelly roll pan.

Tip the dough onto the prepared pan and use your fingers to stretch it out to fill the pan. Cover it lightly with plastic, and let it puff up. It should rise up to about ¼ inch above the edge of the pan. In a small bowl combine the remaining ¼ cup sugar and the cinnamon.

Remove the plastic and without deflating the dough, use your fingers to make dimples all over the surface. Sprinkle half of the sugar mixture evenly over the dough, then the berries, and, finally, the remaining sugar mixture.

Bake until golden brown, puffed, and set, even under the pockets of fruit, 20 to 25 minutes. Drizzle with the remaining 2 tablespoons butter. Let cool slightly in the pan on a rack, then slip the focaccia out of the pan onto a cutting board, cut into 12 pieces, and serve warm.

This focaccia is best the day it's made, but leftover pieces can be stored in an airtight container for up to 2 days. Reheat leftovers in a low oven.

BITTERSWEET CHOCOLATE PUDDING

SERVES 4 TO 6

4 ounces bittersweet chocolate (60 to 70 percent cacao), chopped (about 1 cup)

2 tablespoons unsalted butter

4 large egg yolks, lightly beaten

1/3 cup sugar

1/3 cup (1 ounce) cocoa powder (Dutch-process or natural), sifted

2 tablespoons cornstarch

2 teaspoons ground cinnamon

1/2 teaspoon kosher salt

2 cups whole milk

1 cup heavy cream

2 teaspoons pure vanilla extract

Crème fraîche or fresh whipped cream, for serving

My husband says this is the best dessert I've ever made. I'm not sure how to take that—on the one hand, it's just pudding. On the other hand, I'm not sure that he's wrong. I've done a lot of field research on puddings: I grew up as hooked on those five-letter pudding snacks as anyone. But once you make this pudding from scratch, you'll never go back to the pudding packs. My recipe combines cocoa powder and melted bittersweet chocolate for a deep chocolate flavor and burnished mahogany color. A healthy dose of ground cinnamon adds a familiar warmth that gives this childhood favorite a sophisticated edge. It tastes and looks almost roasted—and it makes store-bought chocolate pudding seem, well, vanilla.

Place the chocolate and the butter in a medium bowl. Set a fine-mesh sieve over the bowl and set aside. Set the egg yolks in another medium bowl.

In a medium saucepan, whisk together the sugar, cocoa powder, cornstarch, cinnamon, and salt. Gradually whisk in the milk and cream. Bring the mixture to a boil over medium heat, whisking constantly, 4 to 5 minutes. Cook until thick and creamy, 1 minute. Carefully ladle about 1/4 cup of the hot milk mixture into the yolks and whisk to combine. Repeat this process a few times until the milk mixture has been incorporated and the pudding is smooth. Return the mixture to the pot and cook over low heat for another 30 seconds to 1 minute.

Immediately strain the custard through the sieve into the bowl, stirring to help it along. Let the pudding stand for 1 minute, then add the vanilla and whisk until smooth. Let the pudding cool slightly then cover it with plastic wrap, making sure the plastic touches the pudding (that will inhibit the formation of a skin).

Serve cold with a dollop of crème fraîche or whipped cream. Store the pudding in the refrigerator, well-wrapped, for up to 3 days.

MAPLE STICKY BUNS

MAKES 8 BUNS

DOUGH

6 tablespoons (¾ stick) unsalted butter, cut into small pieces, plus more for greasing the bowl

⅔ cups whole milk

1 large egg, lightly beaten

2½ cups (11¼ ounces) bread flour, plus more for the work surface, if necessary

3 tablespoons granulated sugar

1¾ teaspoons active dry yeast

½ teaspoon kosher salt

TOPPING

6 tablespoons (¾ stick) unsalted butter, plus more for greasing the pan

¼ cup packed dark brown sugar

¼ cup maple syrup

½ teaspoon kosher salt

2 ounces (½ cup) pecans, coarsely chopped

2 ounces (½ cup) walnuts, coarsely chopped

⅓ cup (1½ ounces) raisins

FILLING

¼ cup packed dark brown sugar

2 tablespoons ground cinnamon

½ teaspoon kosher salt

3 tablespoons unsalted butter, at room temperature

There is a sticky bun debate raging in our house: sticky buns for breakfast or sticky buns for dessert? To me, a traditional sticky bun, with its pumped-up stature and gobs of caramel, seems out of place on the breakfast table. I'm not saying I wouldn't enjoy one first thing in the morning, but I'd likely have to spend the rest of the day lying down. My husband, on the other hand, is a breakfast partisan. For this recipe, I set out to create something we could both eat for breakfast. Something decadent but not gut-busting, classic but fresh. The tender, yeasty bread is adorned with a cap of crunchy nuts, sweet caramel, and a swirl of cinnamon so fragrant you may be able to forego coffee. A little maple syrup adds complex sweetness that belongs at the morning meal.

Lightly grease a large bowl and set aside.

To prepare the dough, in a small pot, bring the milk just to a boil over medium heat. Watch closely to ensure that the milk doesn't boil over. Remove from the heat and add the butter to the pot to melt. Add the mixture to a small bowl and let it cool to 105°F to 110°F. (It should be warm to the touch but not too hot.) Add the egg and stir to combine.

In the bowl of a stand mixer fitted with the paddle attachment, or in a large bowl with a wooden spoon, combine the flour, sugar, yeast, and salt. Add the warm milk mixture and mix just until combined.

Switch to the dough hook and knead the dough on low speed until smooth and elastic, about 6 minutes. Or, tip the dough onto a work surface and knead by hand for about 12 minutes. You shouldn't need to add flour. Form the dough into a ball, put it in the prepared bowl, and cover with plastic wrap. Leave it in a warm, draft-free spot until it has doubled in size. This could take 30 minutes or 2 hours depending on the temperature. Keep an eye on the dough rather than the clock.

CONTINUED

Meanwhile, make the topping. Butter a 9 by 2-inch round cake pan. In a small saucepan, combine the butter, brown sugar, maple syrup, and salt. Cook over medium heat, stirring occasionally, until the mixture reaches a full boil and looks foamy with large bubbles. (It should register 212°F on a candy thermometer.) Pour the caramel into the prepared pan. Sprinkle pecans, walnuts, and raisins evenly over the top. Set aside.

To prepare the filling, mix together the brown sugar, cinnamon, and salt in a small bowl. Cover with plastic wrap and set aside.

When the dough has doubled, tip it out onto a very lightly floured work surface. Knead it once or twice to expel the air and then roll it into a 10-inch square. Spread the 3 tablespoons butter evenly over the surface and sprinkle with the reserved filling. Tightly roll up the dough and pinch the top seam closed. With a serrated knife, cut the roll crosswise into 8 equal pieces. Set them in the pan with the topping, spirals facing upward. Cover loosely with plastic wrap, and let them rest until the dough has almost doubled again, about 1 hour. They should look pillowy and all of the rolls will be touching.

Preheat the oven to 375°F. Uncover the rolls and bake until deep golden brown and puffed, 25 to 30 minutes. (Set a piece of aluminum foil on the rack beneath the buns to catch any caramel that may drip out.) Give the center roll a wiggle—if it's set in place, the buns are ready to come out. If the middle of that center roll feels soft, give them another few minutes. Let cool on a rack for 5 minutes then carefully cut around the edge with a paring knife and invert the rolls onto a serving plate. Let cool slightly before eating, if possible. These are best the day they're made, served warm and gooey.

Store leftovers in an airtight container at room temperature up to 2 days. To reheat them, wrap them in foil and pop them in a low oven until warm.

BLUEBERRY CUSTARD TARTS

MAKES 20 TARTS

PASTRY

2 cups (9 ounces)
all-purpose flour, plus more
for the work surface

½ teaspoon kosher salt

¾ cup (1½ sticks) unsalted
butter, frozen

6 to 8 tablespoons ice water

1 teaspoon ground
cinnamon

FILLING

4 large egg yolks

¼ cup granulated sugar

¾ cup whole milk

¾ cup heavy cream,
plus more for brushing

4 ounces (¾ cup) fresh
blueberries, wild if possible

TO FINISH

2 tablespoons heavy cream

Confectioners' sugar,
for dusting

I loved my time as an intern in the *Saveur* test kitchen. One day I'd be traveling across town with a ham leg the size of my torso so that Jonathan Waxman could slice it perfectly. The next I'd be visiting matzo factories in Queens. No two days were ever the same. On one of my favorite days, I tested a recipe for the most perfect Portuguese custard tarts, filled with pleasantly sour passion fruit and blueberries. So many years and so many desserts later, I still can't get those beauties out of my mind. Classic *pastéis de nata*, invented by Portuguese monks sometime in the nineteenth century, are a national treasure. The baked mini egg custard pies are often dusted with cinnamon when they emerge from the oven, which makes sense, given the Portuguese history of traveling the world in search of spices.

These blueberry custard tarts are my version. I swirled a ribbon of cinnamon throughout the buttery pastry dough instead so that it hits your tongue as soon as you take a bite. Then I filled them with a perfect, creamy, blueberry-studded custard. They're portable, tasty, and cute as a button. If you can find them, use wild blueberries. Since they're small, you can fit more in each tart.

Lightly flour a work surface and have ready two 12-cup nonstick muffin tins.

To prepare the pastry, whisk together the flour and salt in a large bowl. Using the large holes of a box grater, grate the frozen butter over the flour. Add 6 tablespoons of the ice water and stir with a fork until a shaggy dough starts to form. Add up to 2 more tablespoons water if necessary to get the dough to come together, but it shouldn't be too wet. It should just hold together when squeezed.

Tip the dough onto the work surface. With a lightly floured rolling pin, shape the dough into a 12 by 6-inch rectangle with a short side nearest you. Fold the dough into thirds like a letter. (Fold the bottom third up and

CONTINUED

then the top third down over the bottom third.) Rotate the dough so that the folded edge is to the left. Repeat rolling and folding two more times, lightly flouring the surface as necessary to keep the dough from sticking. Wrap the dough tightly with plastic wrap and refrigerate for about 1 hour. Repeat the entire rolling and folding process one more time for a grand total of six turns. Wrap and refrigerate the dough for at least 1 hour. At this point, you can wrap the dough tightly and refrigerate it for up to 2 days or freeze it for up to a month.

On a lightly floured surface, roll the dough into a 15 by 16-inch rectangle. Sprinkle evenly with cinnamon. Tightly roll the dough starting at the long end, and pinch the top seam closed. With a serrated knife, cut the roll into 20 equal pieces. Set the pieces on the work surface with the spirals facing upward. Use your palm to flatten the dough, and then roll each piece into a neat 4-inch circle. Press the dough evenly into the bottom and sides of the muffin tin cups. Push the dough up about ⅛ inch above the edge. Freeze the dough in the tins until completely frozen, at least 1 hour.

Meanwhile, prepare the custard filling. In a medium bowl, whisk together the egg yolks and sugar until pale. In a medium saucepan, heat the milk and cream over medium heat until hot. Slowly add the milk mixture to the yolk mixture while whisking to combine. Set aside.

Preheat the oven to 400°F. Brush the edge of each tart shell with a little bit of cream. Bake the frozen tart shells until set and beginning to brown, 12 to 15 minutes. Decrease the oven temperature to 325°F. You may have to wait a few minutes for the oven to cool down. Place a few blueberries in each shell and then carefully fill with the custard mixture.

Bake until the custard is just set with a slight jiggle in the center, 8 to 12 minutes. Let the tarts cool in the pans on a rack for 5 minutes. Using an offset spatula, remove the tarts from the pans and let cool 15 minutes more. These are really best served warm or at room temperature with a dusting of confectioners' sugar.

CINNAMON, HAZELNUT, AND DATE BUNS

MAKES 1 DOZEN BUNS

DOUGH
6 tablespoons (¾ stick) unsalted butter, plus more for greasing the bowl and the dish

½ cup whole milk

2 tablespoons finely grated orange zest (from 2 oranges)

⅓ cup granulated sugar

2½ teaspoons active dry yeast

1 large egg plus 3 large egg yolks, lightly beaten

3 cups (13½ ounces) all-purpose flour, plus more if needed, and for the work surface

1 teaspoon kosher salt

FILLING
¼ cup boiling water

8 ounces (about 14) Medjool dates, pitted

4 ounces (¾ cup) hazelnuts, toasted and skinned (see page 11)

3 tablespoons unsalted butter, melted

¼ cup packed light brown sugar

3 tablespoons ground cinnamon

½ teaspoon kosher salt

TO FINISH
1 large egg yolk

2 teaspoons water

These buns are bursting with flavor. The exotic combination of cinnamon, hazelnuts, and orange zest creates flavorful, fragrant rolls that will call everyone to the kitchen from all corners of the house. Plump Medjool dates add natural sweetness. The recipe came to me as I was reading about the ancient Arabian traders who dealt in cinnamon. I'd bet they discovered this perfect combination thousands of years before I did. Resist the urge to add too much flour to the dough when kneading; it should be sticky. The results are astonishingly pillowy and tender. They're so irresistible that I always burn myself trying to pull one from the hot pan too soon!

I prefer these buns without glaze, topped with a generous swipe of cream cheese for extra richness. But for glazed buns, simply whisk together 1 cup of confectioners' sugar, 3 tablespoons whole milk, a splash of vanilla extract, and a pinch of salt, and drizzle away.

Lightly butter a large bowl and set aside.

To prepare the dough, in a small pot, bring the milk just to a boil over medium heat. Watch closely to ensure that the milk doesn't boil over. Remove from the heat and add the butter to the pot to melt. Pour the mixture into a small bowl, add the orange zest, and let it cool to 105°F to 110°F. (It should be warm to the touch but not too hot.)

In the bowl of a stand mixer fitted with the paddle attachment, or in a large bowl, combine the milk mixture, sugar, yeast, egg, and yolks on medium speed. With the mixer on low speed, or with a wooden spoon, add 2 cups of the flour then the salt.

If using a mixer, switch to the dough hook, add the remaining 1 cup of flour, and mix on low speed. Slowly add up to ¼ cup more flour if necessary, 1 tablespoon at a time, until the dough is smooth and just pulls away from the sides of the bowl. The dough should still be a little wet and you may not need the entire ¼ cup flour. Knead

CONTINUED

dough on low speed until smooth and elastic, about 6 minutes. Or, tip the dough onto a work surface and knead by hand for about 12 minutes.

Form the dough into a ball, set it in the prepared bowl, and cover with plastic wrap. Leave it in a cozy spot until it has doubled in size. This could take 30 minutes or 2 hours depending on the temperature. Keep an eye on the dough rather than the clock.

Meanwhile, prepare the filling. In a medium bowl, pour the boiling water over the dates and let stand until the dates have softened, about 10 minutes. In a food processor fitted with the metal blade, pulse the hazelnuts until coarsely chopped and tip them out into a small bowl and set aside. To the food processor, add the dates, along with any liquid, and the butter and puree until smooth. Add the brown sugar, cinnamon, and salt and pulse until combined. Butter a 9 by 13-inch baking pan.

Punch down the dough and turn it out onto a very lightly floured surface. With a lightly floured rolling pin, roll it into a 16 by 12-inch rectangle. The dough should feel like heaven in your hands, soft and supple, and it should be easy to work with. Spread the date filling evenly over the entire surface and then sprinkle evenly with the reserved nuts, pressing them gently to adhere. Tightly roll the dough, starting at a short end, and pinch the top seam closed. With a serrated knife, cut the roll crosswise into 12 equal pieces. Set the pieces in the prepared dish, spirals facing upward, cover with plastic wrap, and let rest until the dough is pillowy and the slices are touching, about 1 hour.

Preheat the oven to 350°F. In a small bowl, prepare an egg wash by whisking together the egg yolk and the 2 teaspoons water. Uncover the rolls and brush with the egg wash. Bake until golden brown, 16 to 22 minutes. Invert the rolls onto a wire rack and let cool 10 minutes, then flip onto a serving plate (that is, if they aren't already gone).

These buns are best served warm, but you can store leftovers well wrapped at room temperature for up to 2 days. Warm leftovers in a low oven.

CINNAMON TOAST BREAD PUDDING

SERVES 8

¼ cup (½ stick) unsalted butter, at room temperature, plus more for greasing the dish

2 teaspoons ground cinnamon

6 to 8 slices brioche, cut ½ inch thick

1½ cups heavy cream

1½ cups whole milk

4 large eggs plus 4 large egg yolks

⅔ cup packed light brown sugar

1 teaspoon pure vanilla extract

½ teaspoon kosher salt

Confectioners' sugar, for dusting (optional)

This bread pudding starts with cinnamon butter (which, I should add, is dynamite on its own) slathered on fresh brioche. The brioche is toasted until crisp and caramelized and then baked in a perfect, vanilla-scented custard. Toasting the bread first gives this special pudding character and some crunch around the edges.

Preheat the oven to 350°F. Butter a 2-quart baking dish.

In a small bowl, with a small spoon, combine the butter and cinnamon. Spread the butter mixture on one side of each bread slice and then cut each slice in half crosswise. Put the bread pieces on a baking sheet, butter side up, and bake until golden brown and toasted, 8 to 10 minutes.

In a large bowl, whisk together the cream, milk, eggs, yolks, brown sugar, vanilla, and salt. Arrange the toast in the prepared baking dish, slightly overlapping the pieces to fit, and pour the cream mixture over it. Press the toast down gently, cover it with plastic wrap, and refrigerate for 30 minutes to 1 hour. You want the toast to soak up that luscious custard.

Bring a kettle of water to a boil.

Remove the plastic and set the baking dish in a large roasting pan. Fill the roasting pan with enough boiling water to get about halfway up the sides of the baking dish. Carefully place the pan in the oven and bake until the custard is set (even in the very center), and the bread has puffed, 50 to 60 minutes. Let cool slightly and remove the baking dish from the water.

I prefer this pudding served warm or at room temperature but you can chill it, covered, in the refrigerator for up to 1 day and serve cold with a dusting of confectioners' sugar.

JAGGERY FLAN

SERVES 8

¼ cup water

½ cup granulated sugar

3½ cups whole milk

½ cup heavy cream

¾ cup scraped jaggery or packed dark brown sugar

½ teaspoon ground cinnamon

3 large eggs plus 4 large egg yolks

¼ teaspoon kosher salt

Jaggery is a flavorful sugar made from the sap of coconut or date palms. My father's mother was famous for her *kalu dodol*, a fudge-like candy made with liquid jaggery. She would set a giant cauldron over an open flame in the yard, under the unforgiving tropical sun, and stir the pot for hours until the texture was just right. This process could take up to eight hours.

I've never even considered trying to make *kalu dodol*. Too hot. Too much work. That's my grandmother's territory. But I wouldn't be my father's daughter if I didn't love the wonderful, almost date-like, fruity, deep sweetness of jaggery. That's why I put it in my flan. As opposed to eight hours of stirring, this dessert takes about twenty minutes to pull together.

Look for blocks of jaggery in Asian grocery stores and online. My favorite market keeps the best stuff in the refrigerated section of the store. Jaggery made from sugarcane is more widely available in the US, but I prefer the dark, sticky jaggery from the coconut palm. I encourage you to experiment and use whichever variety tastes the best to you. The flavor and quality of jaggery can vary dramatically, so be sure to take a nibble of a fresh piece before adding it to the custard. If you can't find suitable jaggery, dark brown sugar makes a nice substitute. To measure the jaggery, shave thin flakes off the block with a sharp knife, put the flakes in a measuring cup, and pack them gently. And if you have leftover jaggery, it's heavenly scraped over plain yogurt.

Preheat the oven to 325°F. Have ready an 8 by 2-inch round cake pan and a fine-mesh sieve.

Add the water to a small pot. Pour the granulated sugar into the center so that it is evenly moistened. Cook on medium-high heat, without stirring, until the sugar turns amber, 4 to 6 minutes, swirling the pan to color the mixture evenly. Working quickly, pour the caramel into the cake pan and swirl it to coat the bottom evenly.

In a medium pot, heat the milk, cream, jaggery, and cinnamon over medium heat until hot but not boiling, and the jaggery is dissolved, stirring occasionally. You may need to rub the jaggery against the side of the pot with a wooden spoon to dissolve it.

In a large bowl, whisk together the eggs, egg yolks, and salt. While whisking, gently add about ½ cup of the hot milk mixture to the egg mixture. Continuing to whisk, add another ½ cup, then mix in the remaining milk mixture. Strain the mixture through the fine-mesh sieve into the prepared cake pan. Cover the cake pan with aluminum foil and set it in a large roasting pan. Bring a kettle of water to a boil and add enough boiling water to come halfway up the sides of the pan. Bake until the custard is just set but still jiggles slightly in the center when shaken, 50 to 60 minutes.

Carefully remove the pan from the hot water and let cool on a rack for about 30 minutes. Cover with plastic wrap and chill for at least 4 hours and up to 2 days. To unmold, run a sharp knife around the inside edge of the pan, place a rimmed serving plate upside down over the top, and invert. Keep leftovers in the fridge, well wrapped, for up to 2 days.

PLUM GALETTE WITH HAZELNUT FRANGIPANE

SERVES 8

PASTRY

2 cups (9 ounces)
all-purpose flour, plus more
for the work surface

2 teaspoons sugar

1/2 teaspoon kosher salt

10 tablespoons (1¼ sticks)
cold unsalted butter,
cut into pieces

6 to 8 tablespoons ice water

FILLING

2¼ ounces (½ cup)
hazelnuts, toasted, skinned,
and cooled (see page 11)

¼ cup plus 3 tablespoons
sugar

1 large egg

3 tablespoons unsalted
butter, at room temperature,
cut into pieces

1 tablespoon all-purpose
flour

1 teaspoon ground
cinnamon

½ teaspoon kosher salt

1 pound ripe red or black
plums (about 4 medium),
pitted and cut into ½-inch
wedges

TO FINISH

1 large egg yolk

2 teaspoons water

Sanding sugar, for sprinkling
(optional)

As lovely as this galette is to behold, the pleasure of eating it outweighs its beauty. Golden brown flaky, buttery crust wrapped around roasted plums, soft and fragrant, bursting with purple juices. Under that pleasant mess is a layer of sweet hazelnut frangipane, a creamy nut filling that is mostly soft and luscious but also toothsome like a perfect cookie in spots. Present this to your friends at your next dinner party and the "oohs" and "aahs" will transition quickly to "mmmms."

If you don't have a food processor to grind the nuts, use 2¼ ounces of store-bought hazelnut meal in lieu of the whole nuts.

To make the pastry, whisk together the flour, sugar, and salt in a large bowl. Cut the butter in with a pastry blender or two knives until the mixture resembles even, coarse sand without big pieces (big pieces of butter can melt out in the oven and create holes in the crust of a free-form galette).You can use your fingers to rub the butter into the flour to get a more even distribution, but be sure to chill the mixture for a few minutes before proceeding if the butter has gotten warm. Add 6 tablespoons of the ice water to the mixture and stir with a fork until a shaggy dough forms. Add 1 or 2 more tablespoons of water if you need to, but stop before the dough gets too wet. It should just hold together when squeezed.

Gather the dough into a rough ball in the bowl with your hands. Put a piece of plastic wrap on the counter and place the dough on it. Wrap the dough and flatten it into a 6-inch disk. Refrigerate until cold, about 2 hours or up to 2 days. Alternatively, freeze the dough, well wrapped, for up to 1 month.

Preheat the oven to 400°F.

To make the filling, in a food processor fitted with the metal blade, combine the hazelnuts and ¼ cup of the sugar and pulse until the nuts are finely ground. Be sure to stop

CONTINUED

before you've made a paste. Add the egg, 2 tablespoons of the butter, the flour, cinnamon, and salt and blend until well-combined. Put the mixture in a small bowl. In a medium bowl, toss the plums with the remaining 3 tablespoons sugar.

On a lightly floured, large piece of parchment paper, using a lightly floured rolling pin, roll the dough out to a 13-inch circle. Set the parchment and the dough onto a rimmed baking sheet. If the dough has gotten soft at this point, pop it in the freezer for a few minutes until it becomes firm enough to work with but not frozen. Scoop the hazelnut mixture into the center of the dough. Top the hazelnut mixture with the plums and any accumulated juices, keeping everything centered, leaving a 3 to 4-inch border of dough bare. This mixture will be a bit runny. Do your best to work quickly and keep everything mounded in the center. Fold the bare border of the pastry up and around the filling, moving any runny filling back to the center, and pleating the dough as needed to seal. Put the galette on the sheet in the freezer and freeze for 15 minutes.

In a small bowl, make an egg wash by whisking together the egg yolk and the 2 teaspoons water. Brush the top of the pastry and the edges with the egg wash. Sprinkle with sanding sugar. Top the filling with the remaining 1 tablespoon of butter. Bake until the crust is golden brown, the hazelnut filling is puffed and set, and the plums are tender, 45 to 55 minutes. Let cool slightly on the sheet on a rack before serving.

This tart is really best eaten the day it's made but leftovers can be stored at room temperature for up to 2 days.

RICOTTA CHEESECAKE WITH BOURBON-RAISIN JAM

SERVES 8 TO 10

CRUST

2 cups (about 8 ounces) graham cracker crumbs

6 tablespoons (¾ stick) unsalted butter, melted

2 tablespoons sugar

½ teaspoon kosher salt

FILLING

8 ounces cream cheese, at room temperature

⅓ cup sugar

¾ teaspoon ground cinnamon

Pinch of kosher salt

8 ounces whole-milk ricotta

2 large eggs

JAM

1½ cups water

¾ cup bourbon

1 cup (5¼ ounces) raisins, finely chopped

1 tablespoon sugar

1 (2-inch) cinnamon stick

¼ cup (1 ounce) shelled roasted pistachios, finely chopped

1 tablespoon unsalted butter

Pinch of kosher salt

I'm a New Yorker, and I love my cheesecake. I like it dense. I like it fluffy. But mostly, I like it sooner rather than later. This tart has all the elements of a heavenly cheesecake but takes a fraction of the time. The jam recipe makes a little more than you'll need, but you can slather some of the leftovers on toast or swirl a bit into some oatmeal at breakfast.

Preheat the oven to 350°F. To prepare the crust, combine the graham cracker crumbs, butter, sugar, and salt in a 9-inch fluted tart pan with a removable bottom or a standard 9-inch pie plate. Press the crumbs into the bottom and sides of the pan. Bake the shell on a baking sheet until just beginning to brown, 14 to 16 minutes. Let the shell cool completely on the sheet on a rack.

To prepare the filling, in a large bowl, with an electric mixer on medium-high speed, beat the cream cheese, sugar, cinnamon, and salt until light and fluffy, about 3 minutes. Beat in the ricotta. Add the eggs. Scrape the filling into the prepared tart shell and smooth the top.

Bake the tart on a baking sheet until the filling is set around the edges but still has a slight jiggle in the center, 25 to 30 minutes. Transfer to a rack to cool slightly. Wrap loosely with plastic wrap and refrigerate until completely cool, at least 6 hours and up to 2 days.

To prepare the jam, in a small saucepan, combine the water, bourbon, raisins, sugar, and cinnamon stick. Bring to a simmer over medium heat and cook until the raisins are very soft, about 15 minutes. Add a little more water if the raisins get too dry.

Remove the cinnamon stick and add the raisin mixture to the bowl of a food processor fitted with the metal blade. Add the pistachios, butter, and salt and pulse until a chunky sauce forms. Let cool to room temperature. Serve slices of the chilled tart with a dollop of the raisin jam. Keep leftovers in the fridge, well wrapped, for up to 2 days.

TRUE LOVE CAKE

SERVES 16

¾ cup (1½ sticks) unsalted butter, plus more for greasing the pan

1 cup (6 ounces) coarse semolina

4 large eggs, separated, plus 2 large egg yolks

1⅓ cups sugar

¼ cup honey

1 tablespoon rose water

¾ teaspoon almond extract

2 teaspoons ground cinnamon

1½ teaspoons freshly ground cardamom

1 teaspoon finely grated lemon zest (from 1 lemon)

¾ teaspoon kosher salt

1 cup (4½ ounces) finely chopped raw cashews

This sticky semolina cake is the first cake I ever made in my grandmother's kitchen in Sri Lanka. The fragrant, cashew-studded treat is served throughout the country at teatime or whenever guests come calling. The dense crumb and chewy edges remind me of something that would happen if a butter cake and a blondie had a baby—a pleasingly crunchy, tender, and sweet love child. In the oven, the rose water, honey, cardamom, and cinnamon start to bloom. This cake doubles as aromatherapy.

Preheat the oven to 300°F. Butter a 9-inch square baking pan. Line the pan with parchment paper, leaving a 2-inch overhang on two sides. Butter the parchment.

In a large skillet, melt the butter over medium heat. Add the semolina and cook, stirring, until it is very lightly toasted, 2 to 3 minutes. Turn the semolina mixture out onto a large plate to cool to room temperature.

In a large bowl, with an electric mixer, beat the 6 egg yolks and sugar on medium speed until pale and thick, 3 to 4 minutes. Beat in the honey, rose water, almond extract, cinnamon, cardamom, lemon zest, and salt. Beat in the cooled semolina mixture and fold in the cashews.

With clean beaters, whip the 4 egg whites to medium-stiff but not dry peaks on medium speed, about 2 minutes. Stir one-quarter of the egg whites into the semolina mixture, then fold the remaining egg whites into the batter. Pour the batter into the prepared pan and smooth the top. Bake until golden brown and a toothpick inserted into the center comes out with moist crumbs attached, 40 to 50 minutes. Let cool completely in the pan on a rack. To serve, cut along the edges of the cake to release it from the pan. Using the parchment, transfer the cake to a cutting board and cut into diamonds. Store the cake in an airtight container at room temperature for up to 3 days.

NEW LOVE CAKE

SERVES 10

CAKE

10 tablespoons (1¼ sticks) unsalted butter, melted and cooled slightly, plus more for greasing the pans

1 cup chopped fresh ripe pineapple (from ½ a medium pineapple)

1¼ cups granulated sugar

2 cups (9 ounces) all-purpose flour

1 cup (6 ounces) coarse semolina

1½ tablespoons ground cinnamon

1 tablespoon baking powder

1 tablespoon freshly ground cardamom

¾ teaspoon kosher salt

4 large eggs

½ cup whole milk, at room temperature

1 tablespoon rose water

2 teaspoons finely grated lemon zest (from 1 lemon)

BRITTLE

2 teaspoons unsalted butter, plus more for greasing the sheet

¼ cup granulated sugar

Pinch of cream of tartar

2 tablespoons water

½ cup roasted cashews, coarsely chopped

My grandmother loved to rearrange furniture. Fortunately, there weren't that many items to move around her airy hilltop home. A brown couch. Some rickety chairs. A wooden, white box with her flowering ginger plants. The stone garden bench. After a night's sleep, we would often find that the living room looked completely different than it had the prior evening. I think I know what she was going for. Sure, we loved watching the birds from the garden bench under the frangipani tree, but what magic could we witness if the bench were moved to the other side of the avocado tree?

Traditional love cake (True Love Cake, page 66) has a permanent place in my heart thanks to early cooking classes in my grandmother's kitchen. But she rubbed off on me in more ways than one! Just like her, I can never leave well enough alone. Although the original is perfect as it is, I couldn't help but rearrange the ingredients and create my own version of love cake. I've taken the same distinctive flavors of cinnamon, rose water, and cardamom and reimagined them as a gorgeous layer cake complete with cream cheese frosting, fresh pineapple, and a sweet-and-salty cashew nut brittle. I've fallen hard for this dessert, and I think it just might be a new love for you, too. Now, about that end table...

Preheat the oven to 350°F. Butter two 8-inch round cake pans and line the bottoms of the pans with parchment paper.

To prepare the cake, in a small bowl, toss the pineapple with 1 tablespoon of the sugar. In a large bowl, whisk together the flour, semolina, cinnamon, baking powder, cardamom, and salt. In another large bowl, whisk together the remaining sugar, butter, eggs, milk, and rose water. Add the flour mixture and stir to combine. Fold in the pineapple and lemon zest. Divide the batter evenly between the prepared pans and smooth the top. Bake until golden

FROSTING

2 (8-ounce) packages cream cheese, at room temperature

6 tablespoons (¾ stick) unsalted butter, at room temperature

½ cup confectioners' sugar

Pinch of kosher salt

brown and a toothpick inserted in the center comes out with moist crumbs attached, 30 to 35 minutes. Let the cakes cool in the pans on a wire rack for 5 minutes. Invert the cakes onto a rack and let cool completely.

To prepare the brittle, butter a small baking sheet. In a small saucepan, bring the sugar, cream of tartar, and water to a simmer over medium-high heat. Cook, swirling the pan occasionally, until the sugar is evenly amber-colored, about 5 minutes. Remove from the heat, add the butter and the cashews, and stir to melt the butter and evenly coat the cashews. Pour onto the prepared baking sheet and let cool completely. Once the brittle is cool and hard, move it to a cutting board and coarsely chop.

To prepare the frosting, with an electric mixer, beat the butter and cream cheese on medium-high speed until fluffy, about 3 minutes. Add the confectioners' sugar and salt and beat until smooth.

Place one cooled cake on a serving plate. Spread with about ½ cup of the frosting and top with the other cake layer. Cover the cake with the remaining frosting. Just before serving, sprinkle the brittle on top.

The cake is best the day it's made but will keep, well wrapped at room temperature, for up to 2 days.

SALTED CASHEW CARAMELS

MAKES 64 PIECES

Neutral oil, such as safflower, for the pan

¾ cup heavy cream

¼ cup (½ stick) unsalted butter, cut into pieces

1 cup sugar

½ cup Lyle's Golden Syrup

¼ cup water

5 ounces (1 cup) roasted, salted cashews, coarsely chopped

1½ teaspoons ground cinnamon

½ teaspoon kosher salt

Flaky sea salt, for sprinkling

Cashew nuts grow in the most unexpected way. The fruit of the cashew tree resembles a pear-shaped apple. At the bottom of the red and yellow fruit, a hard, gray cashew-shaped pod grows. This pod contains the cashew kernel, the part we eat. There is a Filipino fable explaining the provenance of the strange appearance of the cashew fruit. According to the tale, the cashew seed began nestled safely inside the fruit. But one day, upon hearing the merrymaking of the creatures in the forest, the cashew nut wished to be outside. A passing fairy, hearing the nut's desperate pleas, granted its wish. After some time on the outside, long after the party was over, the nut realized that the weather in the jungle can be harsh and begged to be back cozy inside the fruit. But the fairy wouldn't grant the wish, insisting that the nut get comfortable with where it was.

Perhaps these cashew nuts could learn to be cozy buried in a chewy caramel? That's where I put them. Cashews and caramel make an excellent pair. The salty nuts are both crunchy and creamy. They punctuate the spiced caramel with bursts of roasted flavor.

Lyle's Golden Syrup (see page 11) is a thick, honey-like syrup made from sugarcane. I use it instead of corn syrup because I prefer its toasty flavor. You can find it in the baking aisle of a well-stocked supermarket, or online.

Lightly oil an 8-inch square baking pan. Line the pan with parchment paper, leaving a 2-inch overhang on two sides. Lightly oil the parchment. Cut sixty-four 3-inch squares of parchment or wax paper for wrapping.

In a small pot, or in a microwave-safe bowl, heat the cream and butter together until melted. (But don't let it boil over!)

Attach a candy thermometer to a medium saucepan and heat the sugar, syrup, and the water over medium-high heat until the sugar turns deep amber and the temperature reaches 310°F, swirling the pan to caramelize

CONTINUED

the sugar evenly, 6 to 8 minutes. In order to get an accurate reading, make sure the bulb of the candy thermometer is submerged in the sugar mixture. You may have to hold the pot tipped to the side while the sugar cooks. Remove from the heat and add the cream mixture. Be careful. This will bubble up and sputter.

Return the pan to the heat. Cook the sugar-cream mixture over medium-high heat until the candy thermometer reads 248°F, 6 to 8 minutes. Stir in the cashews, cinnamon, and salt and pour into the prepared pan. Let cool slightly and refrigerate to harden for about 2 hours.

Using the parchment, lift the block of caramel out of the baking pan and set on a cutting board. Sprinkle with flaky salt and cut into 1-inch squares with a long, sharp knife. Wrap each piece in a square of parchment paper.

The caramels keep their shape best when stored in the fridge. I think they are delicious cold. Bring them back to room temperature before serving, if you prefer.

ALL-EDGES BROWNIE COOKIES

MAKES ABOUT 2 DOZEN COOKIES

1¼ cups (5⅝ ounces) all-purpose flour

¼ cup (¾ ounce) Dutch-process cocoa powder

2½ teaspoons ground cinnamon

¾ teaspoon kosher salt

¼ teaspoon baking soda

½ cup (1 stick) unsalted butter, at room temperature

½ cup granulated sugar

¼ cup packed light brown sugar

1 teaspoon pure vanilla extract

2 large eggs, at room temperature

2¼ ounces bittersweet chocolate (60 to 70 percent cacao), chopped (about ½ cup)

2¼ ounces walnuts, chopped (about ½ cup)

I could eat an entire pan of brownies. Well, okay, I could eat all the edges off an entire pan of brownies. In fact, I've done it. But it makes other people mad, and brownies are supposed to make friends, not enemies. I created this cookie to solve that problem. Toothsome and tender, studded with nuts, chunks of gooey chocolate, and a bold pop of cinnamon, it's my idea of perfect. No wasted middles. No fights. Just chocolate, right in that magical place between crisp, chewy, and soft.

Line two baking sheets with parchment paper.

In a small bowl, whisk together the flour, cocoa powder, cinnamon, salt, and baking soda. In a large bowl, with a wooden spoon, stir the butter, granulated sugar, and brown sugar until creamy, about 2 minutes. Add vanilla and eggs, one a time. Stir in the flour mixture and fold in the chocolate and walnuts. Scoop the dough in 1½ tablespoon balls onto one of the prepared baking sheets and chill until very cold, at least 30 minutes.

Preheat the oven to 325°F.

Using a metal spatula, divide the dough balls between the two prepared sheets, spacing them at least 1½ inches apart. Bake until just set in the center, 12 to 14 minutes, rotating the sheets halfway through. Pull the baking sheets from the oven and tap them gently against the counter a few times to knock the air out of the cookies. Let the cookies cool on the baking sheets, set on racks. Use a metal spatula to release the cookies from the sheets.

They're really best warm, but you can store them in an airtight container at room temperature for 2 days, or in the freezer for up to a month.

nutmeg

By the time I knew my grandmother's sister, Great Auntie Leeda, old age had stolen her hearing and sight and left her a bit unsteady on her feet. The Coke-bottle glasses she wore gave her eyes a bit of a sinister appearance. She was never unkind, but as a wimpy little kid, I kept my distance. Fortunately, it was easy to tell when she was around—a water glass holding her teeth usually sat on a windowsill or tabletop nearby.

Now I wish I had appreciated my time with Auntie Leeda. Apparently, I have her to thank for the generation-skipping baking gene that I inherited. Auntie Leeda's cakes were legendary.

My mother tells me that as a child she loved to visit Leeda, especially at teatime. She recalls driving up the pink gravel path at three in the afternoon, the thought of cake already making her hungry. Auntie Leeda lived in a beautiful, breezy house in Ruwanwella, an hour's drive from Kandy, that must have been a wonderland for kids. Besides the promise of excellent baked goodies, there were also two elephants that lived there and worked on the family's coconut and rubber plantations. On a hot day, my mom, her sister, and her cousins would jump in the nearby shallow stream where the elephants were bathing and scrub the animals' broad backs with heavy ropes made of coconut husks—a cool treat for all parties involved. While the kids frolicked with the animals, Leeda would whip up one of her fabulous cakes and bake it in a portable oven that sat on top of her small gas range.

Leeda's chocolate layer cake was my mother's favorite. No other chocolate cake could match it. It would take years for my mother to discover why—Leeda kept her recipe secrets close. But after she had grown too old to bake, Leeda finally told my mom the secret to her beloved dessert: freshly grated nutmeg. And indeed, it makes a lot of sense that Leeda used nutmeg in her cake; nutmeg trees grew around her house. The dense Sri Lankan jungle, with its moist tropical heat, bright sun, and rich soil, created the perfect conditions for her trees to thrive. Once grown, a nutmeg tree can produce up to one thousand fruits annually for thirty to seventy years. That's a lot of spice for a lot of cakes!

I was very young when we visited Leeda at her home. I spent most of my time scampering around the giant rocks in the yard and the damp forest, swatting mosquitoes, and waiting eagerly to be called to lunch, rather than trying to learn her baking secrets.

But my outdoor explorations did give me a unique appreciation of nutmeg. Imagine me as a small child, playing with a fruit that had fallen from a nutmeg tree. I'd work a crack in the skin and split it open to reveal the nutmeg seed inside, wrapped with a lacy web of red mace. It smelled like cookies baking in heaven—a wonderful surprise for the amateur field botanist. I can see why medieval writers equated the smell of nutmeg and other spices with the smell of paradise, and why profiteering merchants and powerful empires guarded their access to it so jealously. Nutmeg was a key part of their recipe for global wealth and power.

THE NUTMEG TRAIL

Nutmeg is native to the Banda Islands, a cluster of tiny islands in the southeast corner of the Indonesian archipelago. For centuries, the only people who traded with the islands' inhabitants were Arab, Chinese, and Malay merchants, who told their customers tall tales to keep nutmeg's true origin a mystery (and thus ensure high prices). And so stories of cannibals and headhunters guarding the island, or of fierce crocodiles filling treacherous rivers, became part of the spice's allure. Each time nutmeg changed hands along the spice routes through India, Arabia, Persia, and Egypt, it doubled in price. By the time it reached Western Europe, the cost was significant. But even so, by the twelfth century, nutmeg was used all over Europe, as far north as Scandinavia. Not only did its warm scent and flavor carry the experience of paradise, but some believed that nutmeg could be used as protection against the plague. A limited supply and a growing, and often desperate, demand made nutmeg one of the most valued commodities in the world. By the fourteenth century, one pound of nutmeg brought a price of seven fat oxen.

Just how prized was nutmeg? In the seventeenth century, the world's most powerful empires, the Dutch and the British—upstart empires that were increasingly edging out the Spanish and the Portuguese for control of the spice islands and the global trade in spices—spent decades waging battle over the tiny Bandanese Island of Run.

In 1602, the newly established Dutch East India Company signed a treaty with the chiefs of the Banda Islands, securing for the Dutch exclusive rights to buy all the nutmeg grown on all of the Banda Islands except one. The monopoly was strictly enforced, often by violent means. The Dutch burned nutmeg groves belonging to some Bandanese villagers who sold their spice to rival merchants, and killed and enslaved others. After the Bandanese were viciously subdued, the only challengers to Dutch control of the world supply of nutmeg were the English, who had maintained control of an older spice outpost on the tiny island of Run.

Run is only two miles long and less than a mile wide, but it was then a wonderland of nutmeg trees, which flourished even on the island's steep cliffs. The Dutch, eager to maintain their solid monopoly over the global nutmeg market, made claims on the island. The English and the Dutch fought bitterly for control of the island, making and breaking truces and treaties, passing control of Run back and forth.

After years of mutually destructive battles, the rivals came up with an interesting solution to their dispute. In 1667, they solemnized the Treaty of Breda. The treaty gave the Dutch the global monopoly on nutmeg they so valued. And what they gave up in return had cost them very little to begin with, though they had since come to value it very highly. By the terms of the treaty, the British relinquished all claims to the spice island of Run in exchange for a slightly bigger island in the Atlantic Ocean: Manhattan.

Everyone knows that the Dutch acquired Manhattan in exchange for beads. But then, not long afterward, they traded it for control of all the nutmeg in the world.

WHAT IS NUTMEG?

The spice we know as nutmeg is the kernel of the seed of the fruit of the tropical tree *Myristica fragrans*. Its shiny leaves are similar to that of a laurel; its fleshy, yellow edible fruit is similar in shape and size to an apricot. Originally native to the Banda Islands of Indonesia, the tree now also grows in Penang, Sri Lanka, Sumatra, and the West Indies. When the fruit is ripe, it splits to reveal the seed. The bright red, lacy aril surrounding the seed is dried, ground, and sold as mace. To harvest the nutmeg spice, the seed is dried until its shell hardens and the kernel inside—what we grate for use—rattles. Once removed from the shell, the nutmeg kernel is ready for use.

BUYING AND STORING

While ground nutmeg is readily available, I prefer to buy whole unbroken nutmeg kernels and grate them with a fine-toothed kitchen grater as needed. The flavor of freshly grated nutmeg is far superior to ground, which can be stale and dusty. Kept in an airtight container, the whole nutmegs will last much longer than the ground spice.

If you can't find whole nutmeg, ground will work in a pinch. Fresh nutmeg is much more flavorful than ground nutmeg, so you may need a bit more of the ground spice to get the same effect. Ground nutmeg loses its flavor very quickly, so be sure to replace jars often. As a good test, rub some of the spice between your fingertips before using it. If it smells nice, proceed with the recipe. If it doesn't, toss it and buy some whole nutmeg.

CHOCOLATE CAKE FOR LEEDA

SERVES 16

CAKE

⅔ cup melted coconut
oil, plus more for greasing
the pan

1½ cups (6¾ ounces)
all-purpose flour

⅔ cup (2 ounces) natural
cocoa powder

1 tablespoon freshly
grated nutmeg

1 teaspoon ground
cinnamon

¾ teaspoon baking powder

¾ teaspoon baking soda

¾ teaspoon kosher salt

1 cup sugar

2 large eggs, lightly beaten,
at room temperature

2 teaspoons pure
vanilla extract

1 cup whole milk,
at room temperature

FROSTING

8 ounces bittersweet
chocolate (60 to 70 percent
cacao), chopped (about
2 cups)

1 cup heavy cream

½ teaspoon kosher salt

When my mom talks about my Great Aunt Leeda's magical chocolate cake, she closes her eyes, delighted just by the memory. I'm sure I would have loved it as much as she did, but unfortunately I never got to try it. Leeda was careful to keep her best recipes a secret, and no written recipe exists, as far as I know. Here's my best shot at recreating her masterpiece. I used coconut oil instead of butter because it's a good bet that she did, too, living on a coconut-laden island. Plus, it adds moisture and a heavenly tropical essence to the downy cake. These days, coconut oil is easy to find in most supermarkets, right next to the olive and vegetable oils. Mom said that Leeda topped the cake with a simple buttercream made with confectioners' sugar and cocoa powder, but I prefer the richer chocolate taste of a classic chocolate ganache.

Preheat the oven to 350°F. Oil a 9-inch square baking pan and line with parchment paper, leaving a 2-inch overhang on two sides. Lightly oil the parchment.

To prepare the cake, in a medium bowl, whisk together the flour, cocoa powder, nutmeg, cinnamon, baking powder, baking soda, and salt. If your cocoa powder has a few lumps you can sift this mixture, but it isn't necessary otherwise.

In a large bowl, whisk together the coconut oil, sugar, eggs, and vanilla. Whisk in about half of the flour mixture. Then whisk in half of the milk. Repeat this process, stirring until the batter is smooth. Pour the batter into the prepared pan and smooth the top. Tap the pan against the counter a few times to knock out the air bubbles.

Bake until a toothpick inserted into the center comes out with moist crumbs attached, 25 to 30 minutes. Let cool completely on a rack.

To prepare the frosting, place the chocolate in a large bowl. In a small saucepan, bring the cream to a boil. Immediately

CONTINUED

pour it over the chocolate and let stand 1 minute, then whisk until smooth. Let the mixture cool at room temperature to a spreadable consistency, stirring occasionally.

Lift the cake out of the pan and set it on a serving plate. Remove the parchment. Spread the frosting evenly over the top of the cake.

This cake is best the day it's made but you can keep leftovers, well wrapped, at room temperature for 1 day.

HONEYED CASHEW LACE COOKIES

MAKES ABOUT 2 DOZEN COOKIES

7 ounces (1½ cups) unsalted cashews, toasted

⅓ cup (1½ ounces) all-purpose flour

2 teaspoons freshly grated nutmeg

½ teaspoon kosher salt

½ cup packed light brown sugar

¼ cup (½ stick) unsalted butter

2 tablespoons honey

1 tablespoon water

There is a town in Sri Lanka halfway between the ocean and the mountains called Cadjugama, which means "cashew village" in Sinhalese. The irony is that cashews aren't actually grown there, just sold in thatched-roof roadside stalls manned by lovely Sri Lankan ladies with neatly braided hair and brightly colored saris. We would stop in the village whenever we drove through, chat with the ladies, and buy a few bags of roasted cashews for the drive. Well before we got there, my grandmother would be telling us about the gorgeous women of Cadjugama, the most beautiful in all of Sri Lanka. My brother, a handsome, eligible bachelor from the time he turned seventeen (according to my grandmother), always joked about slowing the car down so he could try to find himself a wife.

These cookies are breathtakingly thin and crisp, with a buttery bite that will keep you coming back for more. I use honey as opposed to corn syrup; it adds a lovely floral note.

Preheat the oven to 350°F. Line two baking sheets with parchment paper. In a food processor fitted with the metal blade, pulse the cashews until finely chopped. Put the nuts in a medium bowl and add the flour, nutmeg, and salt.

In a small saucepan, combine the brown sugar, butter, honey, and water over medium heat, stirring, until the mixture has just come to a boil, 2 to 5 minutes. Add it to the cashew mixture and stir to combine.

Working in batches, using a 1-tablespoon measuring spoon, make level scoops and place the mounds of dough on the prepared baking sheets, at least 2 inches apart. Bake until golden brown around the edges, 8 to 10 minutes, rotating the sheets halfway through. Let the cookies cool on the sheets on racks for about 5 minutes then, with a spatula, place the cookies on racks to cool completely.

The cookies are best the day they're made, but store leftovers in an airtight container at room temperature for up to 3 days or in the freezer for up to a month.

BANANA FRITTERS

MAKES ABOUT 2½ DOZEN FRITTERS

½ cup sugar

4 teaspoons freshly grated nutmeg

2 very ripe, small bananas, minced (about ¾ cup)

¾ cup buttermilk

1¾ cups (7⅞ ounces) all-purpose flour

¾ teaspoon baking powder

¼ teaspoon kosher salt

Vegetable oil, for frying

3 large egg whites

In 2006, I spent a wonderful, lazy week under a palm-thatched cabana on an island beach in Thailand with my dear friend Cate. Every day was exactly the same. We breakfasted by the ocean and then set up camp in the hut, reading, swimming, and feeling like the luckiest girls on the planet. Even luckier when four o'clock rolled around and we ordered our daily dose of tea and banana fritters.

There is nothing better than sharing banana fritters with a friend. These cuties fry up so puffy and fragrant that it is in your best interest to invite a few friends over before you let yourself get carried away. A freshly fried mound of hot fritters, soft and banana-flecked, will be gone in minutes.

Line a plate with two layers of paper towels. In a large bowl, combine ¼ cup of the sugar and 1 teaspoon of the nutmeg and set aside. In another large bowl, with a rubber spatula, gently fold together the bananas, buttermilk, the remaining ¼ cup sugar, and the remaining 1 tablespoon of nutmeg. Without mashing the bananas, fold in the flour, baking powder, and salt.

Add the oil to a heavy-bottomed pot. You should have about ¾ inch of oil. Attach a candy thermometer to the side of the pot and bring the oil to 350°F over medium-high heat.

In a medium bowl, beat the egg whites until you have medium-stiff, but not dry, peaks, about 2 minutes. Gently fold the egg whites into the banana mixture.

Using a large spoon or a small cookie scoop, gently drop about 1 rounded tablespoon of the batter into the oil at a time. Add a few more but don't crowd the pan. (Adjust the heat as necessary while frying to keep the temperature at 350°F.) Fry the fritters until golden brown and puffed, about 2 minutes a side, and then, with a slotted spoon, move them to the prepared plate to drain for about 30 seconds. Toss the warm fritters in the nutmeg-sugar mixture and serve hot. Repeat with the remaining batter.

ROASTED PEACH AND BUTTERMILK PIE

SERVES 8 TO 10

PASTRY

1¾ cups (7⅞ ounces) all-purpose flour, plus more for the work surface

1 tablespoon sugar

½ teaspoon kosher salt

½ cup (1 stick) cold unsalted butter, cut into pieces

5 to 7 tablespoons cold buttermilk

1 large egg white, lightly beaten

FILLING

1 pound peaches (2 to 3 large), peeled, pitted, and cut into ¼-inch slices (3 cups sliced)

5 tablespoons unsalted butter

⅔ cup plus 1 teaspoon sugar

2 tablespoons all-purpose flour

2 teaspoons freshly grated nutmeg, plus more for sprinkling

¼ teaspoon kosher salt

4 large eggs, at room temperature

1 cup buttermilk, at room temperature

½ cup heavy cream, at room temperature

TO FINISH (OPTIONAL)

¾ cup heavy cream

1 tablespoon confectioners' sugar

The ripe fruit of the nutmeg tree resembles a peach—both are split by a similar cleft around the center. So it makes a certain kind of sense that nutmeg and peaches make a perfect pair in this tangy, cool, buttermilk custard. This pie is extra-special because it creates lovely layers as it bakes. On top, there is a fluffy cake-like tier, while the bottom is smooth and dotted with peaches. In a pinch, thawed frozen peaches work well in this recipe.

To bake the perfect custard pie, the trick is to know when to pull it from the oven. The recipe timing is a good guide, but your eyes are a much more important tool. Take the pie out when the edges are set and the top of the center is just set but still has quite a bit of jiggle.

To prepare the pastry, whisk together the flour, sugar, and salt in a large bowl. Cut the butter in with a pastry blender or two knives until the mixture resembles coarse meal with a few pea-size pieces. Add 5 tablespoons of the buttermilk and stir with a fork until a shaggy dough starts to form. Add 1 to 2 more tablespoons buttermilk if you need to, but stop before the dough gets too wet. It should just hold together when you squeeze it in your hand.

Gather the dough into a rough ball in the bowl with your hands. Put a piece of plastic wrap on the counter and set the dough on it. Wrap the dough and flatten it into a 6-inch disk. Refrigerate until cold, about 2 hours or up to 2 days. Alternatively, freeze the dough, well wrapped, for up to 1 month.

Have a standard 9-inch glass pie plate ready. Preheat the oven to 425°F.

On a lightly floured surface, using a lightly floured rolling pin, roll the disk of pastry out to about a 13-inch circle that is ⅛ inch thick. Carefully set the dough in the pie plate, easing it into the bottom and sides. Trim off the excess dough, leaving a ¾-inch overhang. Roll the excess dough under to create an even rim and crimp the edges in whatever decorative pattern you like. Chill the crust until firm, about 30 minutes, then freeze for 15 minutes before baking.

Meanwhile, to prepare the filling, in an 8-inch square baking dish, spread the peaches in an even layer. Dot with 1 tablespoon of the butter and sprinkle with 1 teaspoon of the sugar. Roast the peaches in the oven until very soft and silky and browned in spots, stirring halfway through, about 50 minutes. Let cool slightly in the baking dish.

Set the frozen pie shell on a baking sheet and prick the bottom with a fork a few times. Line the shell with parchment paper and fill it with pie weights or dried beans. Bake until the bottom crust underneath the pie weights is dry and set, 15 to 20 minutes. Carefully lift one side of the parchment and weights to peek underneath as needed. Remove the parchment and the pie weights and bake until the crust is golden brown, another 10 to 15 minutes. Remove the pie shell from the oven and immediately brush the bottom and sides of the crust with a light coat of the egg white. Let the crust cool to room temperature. Decrease the oven temperature to 325°F.

Melt the remaining ¼ cup butter and let cool slightly. In a large bowl, whisk together the remaining ⅔ cup sugar with the flour, nutmeg, and salt. Stir in the melted butter, eggs, buttermilk and the cream. Spread the peaches and any accumulated juices along the bottom of the pie shell in an even layer, then pour the buttermilk mixture on top. Transfer the pie on a baking sheet to the oven.

After about 35 minutes, check the pie. It's finished when the top is light golden brown, the edges are set, the top of the center is just set, but the center still jiggles quite a bit. This should take about 45 to 50 minutes. Let the pie cool on a rack for about an hour then refrigerate to cool completely, about 4 to 6 hours.

To serve, whip the cream and confectioners' sugar until soft peaks form. Top the pie with the whipped cream and grate some extra nutmeg on top. Store leftovers well wrapped in the refrigerator for up to 2 days.

CONCORD GRAPE STREUSEL CAKE

SERVES 8 TO 10

STREUSEL

3 tablespoons unsalted
butter, at room temperature
(but not too soft), plus more
for greasing the pan

1/3 cup (1 1/2 ounces)
all-purpose flour

2 tablespoons light
brown sugar

1/4 teaspoon baking powder

1/4 teaspoon freshly
grated nutmeg

Pinch of kosher salt

1 1/2 ounces (1/2 cup)
sliced almonds

CAKE

1 1/2 cups (6 3/4 ounces)
all-purpose flour

1 tablespoon freshly
grated nutmeg

1 teaspoon baking powder

1/2 teaspoon kosher salt

1/2 cup (1 stick) unsalted
butter, at room temperature

3/4 cup packed light
brown sugar

2 large eggs plus 1 large egg
yolk, at room temperature

1/2 teaspoon pure
almond extract

1/3 cup buttermilk,
at room temperature

2 cups (12 1/2 ounces)
Concord grapes, halved
and seeded

Concord grapes are so wonderfully strong that I can often smell them in the farmers' market before I can even see them. They are worth seeking out. You do have to remove the seeds, which sounds like a pain, but really it's no big deal. Slice each grape in half, then, using the tip of your knife, pick the seeds out and discard them. (Don't worry if the skin separates from the flesh. Just be sure to save both parts.) You'll be rewarded with a lovely, tender cake filled with jammy pockets of sweet-tart roasted grape. It makes a nice breakfast too, with a dollop of yogurt.

Preheat the oven to 350°F. Butter a 9-inch springform pan. To prepare the streusel, whisk together the flour, brown sugar, baking powder, nutmeg, and salt in a medium bowl. Using your fingers, knead the butter in until the flour is evenly moistened. Stir in almonds. Set aside.

To prepare the cake, whisk together the flour, nutmeg, baking powder, and salt. In a large bowl, with an electric mixer, beat the butter and brown sugar on medium speed until fluffy, 3 to 4 minutes. Beat in the eggs and egg yolk, one at a time, using a rubber spatula to scrape down the edges of the bowl occasionally. Beat in the almond extract.

Add half of the flour mixture to the butter mixture and beat to combine. Add the buttermilk and beat until smooth, then add the remaining flour mixture and beat just until combined. Pour the batter into the prepared pan and smooth the top. Sprinkle the grapes evenly over the top and press them into the batter very slightly. Gather pieces of streusel dough in your fingers, squeezing it to make clumps, and sprinkle the streusel over the top.

Bake the cake until a toothpick inserted into the center comes out with moist crumbs attached and the streusel is golden brown, 30 to 35 minutes. Let cool slightly on a rack and then remove the pan edge. Serve warm or at room temperature. Store leftovers in an airtight container at room temperature for up to 2 days.

MAPLE-GLAZED PECAN COOKIES

MAKES ABOUT 2 DOZEN COOKIES

COOKIES
½ cup (1 stick) unsalted butter, at room temperature

6 tablespoons granulated sugar

2 large egg yolks

1¼ cups (5⅝ ounces) all-purpose flour

½ teaspoon freshly grated nutmeg

¼ teaspoon baking powder

¾ teaspoon kosher salt

3 ounces (¾ cup) chopped pecans

GLAZE
1 teaspoon unsalted butter, melted

1 tablespoon maple syrup, preferably Grade B

¼ teaspoon freshly grated nutmeg

¼ cup confectioners' sugar

2 to 3 teaspoons water

I'm a sucker for anything with real maple syrup. I'm originally from New England, after all. These cookies are simple, buttery, studded with pecans, spiced with nutmeg, and drizzled with just enough maple glaze to feel cozy and decadent.

To prepare the cookies, beat the butter and the sugar in a large bowl with an electric mixer on medium speed until fluffy, 3 to 4 minutes. Add the egg yolks and beat until combined. Beat in the flour, nutmeg, baking powder, and salt. Add the pecans and beat just until evenly distributed.

Tip the dough out onto a sheet of parchment paper approximately 18 by 13 inches and form it into a rough log shape. Fold the parchment over the dough. Place the long side of a ruler against the bottom edge of the log on top of the parchment. While pressing firmly on the ruler, pull the top layer of the parchment toward you until you have a smooth, 1½ to 2-inch cylinder. Tuck the ends of the parchment over and twist the ends to seal. Freeze the log until solid, at least 4 hours.

Preheat the oven to 350°F. Line two baking sheets with parchment paper. Cut ¼-inch slices from the frozen dough log. Place slices on the prepared sheets about 1 inch apart and bake until set and light golden around the edges, 15 to 18 minutes, rotating the sheets halfway through. Let the cookies cool completely on a rack.

To prepare the glaze, whisk together the melted butter, maple syrup, and nutmeg. Add the confectioners' sugar and enough water to make a smooth, fluid glaze. Drizzle the cookies with the glaze and let stand at room temperature until set. Store the cookies in an airtight container at room temperature for up to 5 days or in the freezer for up to a month.

SPICED COFFEE CUSTARD

SERVES 4

2 cups heavy cream

1 cup whole milk

1 tablespoon freshly grated nutmeg, plus more for sprinkling

4 large egg yolks

¼ cup sugar

4 teaspoons instant espresso powder

Pinch of kosher salt

I started drinking coffee at a young age. The way Sri Lankans make it, with plenty of sugar and creamy milk, it had real kid appeal. Instead of giving me an entire cup, my dad would tip a little of his hot coffee into his saucer for me. Like a caffeine-hungry kitten, I would slurp it up.

These puddings have all the same appeal as those saucers of coffee did back them. Cool, sweet, and smooth coffee-flavored custard with a hint of spice. If you want to be cheeky, you can use pretty ovenproof coffee mugs or teacups instead of ramekins.

Preheat the oven to 325°F. Have ready four 6- to 8-ounce ramekins set in a metal baking pan. Bring a kettle of water to a boil and set aside.

In a small saucepan, combine 1½ cups of the heavy cream, the milk, and the nutmeg over medium-high heat. Cook until bubbles form around the edge of the pan, just before boiling, stirring occasionally. Remove the pot from the heat.

Whisk together the egg yolks, sugar, espresso powder, and salt. Add some of the hot cream mixture to the yolk mixture while whisking. Repeat this process a few times until the two are completely combined. Divide the custard mixture evenly among the ramekins. Add enough boiling water to come halfway up the sides of the ramekins. Cover the pan with aluminum foil and bake until the custards are just set but still jiggle when nudged, 25 to 30 minutes. (Keep an eye on them; you might have to take some out before the others are done.)

Use tongs to transfer the ramekins from the hot water to a rack to cool. Empty the baking pan of water and let cool. Set the ramekins back in the pan, wrap well with plastic wrap, and refrigerate at least 6 hours or up to 2 days. To serve, whip the remaining ½ cup of cream to soft peaks. Top each custard with some whipped cream and a sprinkle of nutmeg.

CAZUELA COOKIE BARS

MAKES 24 BARS

COOKIE BASE
¾ cup (1½ sticks) unsalted butter, at room temperature, plus more for greasing the pan

½ cup packed light brown sugar

½ teaspoon kosher salt

2½ cups (11¼ ounces) all-purpose flour

FILLING
1 cup roasted sweet potato flesh, from 1 medium sweet potato (about 12 ounces)

1 cup pumpkin puree (not pumpkin pie filling)

1 cup coconut milk

½ cup heavy cream

⅔ cup packed light brown sugar

4 teaspoons freshly grated nutmeg

¾ teaspoon ground cinnamon

½ teaspoon kosher salt

4 large eggs

When my father was growing up in Sri Lanka, he had a garden that sounds like something out of a fairy tale—complete with wild pumpkin patch. The curly pumpkin vines grew with such vigor that space became an issue. The only solution was to train them to grow up the sides of the garage and onto the roof. The bright orange orbs would swell and sweeten on the roof, which I imagine was quite a sight. His prolific pumpkins were the inspiration for these bars.

Cazuela is a traditional Puerto Rican baked pudding made with coconut milk, pumpkin, and sweet potato. I decided to pour my version of the creamy orange filling over a thick, crunchy, buttery shortbread cookie. The sturdy crust makes it possible to enjoy a piece with a fork at a more formal dinner or out of hand at a picnic in your favorite garden.

Preheat the oven to 350°F. Lightly butter a 13 by 9-inch baking pan and line with parchment paper so that you have 2 inches overhang on the two long sides.

To prepare the base, with an electric mixer, beat the butter and sugar in a large bowl on medium speed until fluffy, 3 to 4 minutes. Add the salt and flour and beat just until the flour is evenly moistened and the mixture is the texture of a coarse meal. Tip the crumbs into the prepared pan and press down into an even layer. The bottom of a small measuring cup is a great tool for this job.

Bake the base until it is light golden brown and set, 20 to 24 minutes. Let it cool on a rack while you prepare the filling.

To prepare the filling, add the sweet potato, pumpkin, coconut milk, heavy cream, sugar, nutmeg, cinnamon, and salt to the bowl of a food processor fitted with the metal blade and blend until very smooth, scraping down the sides of the bowl as necessary. Add the eggs and process just until combined. Do not overmix.

Pour the sweet potato mixture onto the prepared crust and bake until the filling is set with a slight jiggle in the center, 35 to 45 minutes. Cool for about an hour on a rack, then cover and refrigerate until completely cold, at least 3 hours.

To serve, cut around the edges to loosen them from the pan then use the parchment overhang to lift the uncut bars out of the pan and onto a cutting board. Using a long, sharp knife, slice into bars.

Keep these well wrapped in the fridge for up to 3 days. The crust will start to soften after a day or two in the fridge, but the bars will still be tasty.

FROZEN EGGNOG POPS

MAKES 10 POPS

1½ cups heavy cream

1½ cups whole milk

4 large egg yolks

⅓ cup sugar

1 tablespoon freshly grated nutmeg

⅛ teaspoon kosher salt

1 tablespoon bourbon

1 tablespoon dark rum

In the early sixteenth century, nutmeg became so popular that people in Portugal strung it around their necks and carried graters wherever they went. Not only was it a fashionable sign of wealth, it was also thought to ward off disease. I think we should bring this fashion back. If we had nutmeg on us at all times, eggnog would be practical anytime, too. It's just too delicious to limit to the winter holidays. A good "nog," as we call it around our house, can brighten up any day between October and April. As for May to September, that's what these eggnog pops are for—making the summer merry.

Set a fine-mesh sieve over a large liquid measuring cup. Have ready ten 3-ounce ice pop molds and ten ice pop sticks.

In a medium saucepan, whisk together the cream, milk, egg yolks, sugar, nutmeg, and salt; cook over medium heat, stirring constantly, until just thick enough to coat the back of a spoon, 3 to 5 minutes. If you can draw a clear line through the mixture on the back of a wooden spoon that holds, it's done. Strain the mixture through the sieve into the cup. Stir in the bourbon and rum.

Fill the molds, cover, add sticks, and freeze at least 12 hours. To release the pops, run the bottom of the mold under warm water very briefly.

Serve right away or store individually in small, resealable plastic bags for up to 2 weeks.

GOLDEN SYRUP AND BERRY PUDDING CAKE

SERVES 8

10 tablespoons (1¼ sticks) unsalted butter, at room temperature, plus more for greasing the pan

1 lime

½ cup Lyle's Golden Syrup

4 teaspoons freshly grated nutmeg

2 cups (9 ounces) all-purpose flour

1½ teaspoons baking powder

½ teaspoon kosher salt

⅓ cup packed dark brown sugar

3 large eggs, at room temperature

½ cup whole milk, at room temperature

¾ cup (about 3¼ ounces) raspberries

¾ cup (about 3¼ ounces) blackberries

Vanilla ice cream, for serving

Before Lyle's Golden Syrup (the British pantry staple made from sugarcane, see page 11) was available in the US, my father used to bring it back from Sri Lanka in his suitcase. As far as I know, that dubious plan never backfired. My father always had a supply to drizzle on whatever he was about to eat, from cake to plain white rice. I created this cake, inspired by the traditional British treacle sponge, for him—and I put the syrup inside. There is something so cozy about a steamed cake—like a cute little package, just waiting to be unwrapped. Steaming the cake makes the nutmeg and lime blossom and renders the crumb ultratender and moist. It would be lovely served with the classic light custard sauce crème anglaise, but the American in me always wants good-old-fashioned vanilla ice cream. The cold ice cream with the warm, soft cake and tangy berries is nothing but out of this world.

Preheat the oven to 400°F. Butter a 1½-quart baking dish that is at least 3 inches deep. Grate the zest of the lime and set it aside. Bring a kettle of water to a boil.

Squeeze 1 tablespoon of lime juice into a small bowl. Add the syrup and 1 tablespoon of the nutmeg and whisk to combine. Pour the syrup mixture into the bottom of the prepared dish.

In a small bowl, whisk together the flour, baking powder, salt, and remaining 1 teaspoon of nutmeg. In a large bowl, with an electric mixer, beat the butter, brown sugar, and reserved lime zest on medium speed until fluffy, 3 to 4 minutes. Beat in the eggs, one at a time, until combined. Beat in half of the flour mixture, then the milk, and then the rest of the flour mixture until smooth. Gently fold in the berries. The batter will be thick. Drop the batter in dollops around the dish and then spread it evenly.

Cover the dish with a piece of parchment paper and secure it with a rubber band or butcher's twine. Then cover it with aluminum foil and seal the edges tightly. Set the baking dish in a large pot or a roasting pan with high sides and add enough boiling water to reach halfway up the sides of the dish.

Bake until the cake is set and a skewer inserted into the center of the cake (lift the parchment and the foil to check) comes out with moist crumbs attached, about 90 minutes, adding more boiling water as necessary to maintain the level.

Carefully remove the dish from the hot water and set it on a rack to cool for 5 minutes. Run a knife around the edge of the cake and carefully invert it onto a serving plate. Make sure to get all of that delicious syrup from the bottom of the baking dish.

This cake is best served warm with a scoop of vanilla ice cream. Store leftovers in the fridge, well wrapped, for up to 2 days. The cake will harden up a bit in the fridge but will soften slightly if heated in the microwave or the oven.

BLACKBERRY-PEACH HAND PIES

MAKES 1 DOZEN HAND PIES

PASTRY

2 cups (9 ounces)
all-purpose flour, plus more
for the work surface

¾ teaspoon kosher salt

1¼ cups (2½ sticks)
cold unsalted butter,
cut into ¼-inch pieces

6 to 8 tablespoons ice water

FILLING

¼ cup granulated sugar

4 teaspoons cornstarch

1 teaspoon freshly
grated nutmeg

½ teaspoon ground
cinnamon

Pinch of kosher salt

2 cups (10 ounces)
blackberries, diced small

1 medium peach (about
5 ounces) peeled, pitted,
and finely diced (thawed,
drained, and finely diced
if frozen)

TO FINISH

1 large egg yolk, lightly
beaten

2 teaspoons water

GLAZE

½ cup confectioners' sugar

4 ounces cream cheese,
at room temperature

1 teaspoon pure
vanilla extract

2 to 3 tablespoons whole
milk, at room temperature

You may think it doesn't get better than plain old pie—but with hand pies you get double the puff pastry crust (and you don't have to share). They are also really easy to wrap up and pop into your purse to surprise your unsuspecting friends.

I have a little secret. Unless I can get the most spectacular, in-season peaches, I prefer to use frozen. They've been picked at their peak, they're already peeled and sliced, and they're reliably sweet and delicious. Frozen peaches make it easy to cut back on sugar and let the fruit and spice shine. For these pies, use 5 ounces of thawed frozen peaches in place of 1 medium peach.

To prepare the pastry, combine the flour, salt, and butter pieces in a large bowl. (Make sure the butter pieces are ¼ inch or smaller.) Add 6 tablespoons of the water and mix with a fork just until the dough comes together. Add 1 to 2 more tablespoons water if you need to, but stop before the dough gets too wet. Turn the mixture out onto a lightly floured work surface. It should just hold together when you squeeze it in your hand. With a lightly floured rolling pin, shape the dough into a 12 by 6-inch rectangle with a short side nearest you.

Fold the dough into thirds like a letter. (Fold the bottom third up and then the top third down over the bottom third.) Use a bench scraper to help lift and fold the dough if necessary. At this point, the dough will be very rough and shaggy. As you roll and fold the dough it will come together. Rotate the dough so that the folded edge is to the left. Repeat rolling and folding two more times, lightly flouring the surface as necessary. Wrap the dough tightly with plastic wrap and refrigerate for at least 1 hour. Repeat the entire process one more time for a grand total of six turns. Wrap the dough well and refrigerate until cold, about 4 hours or up to 2 days. Alternatively, freeze the dough, well wrapped, for up to 1 month.

CONTINUED

Line a baking sheet with parchment paper. Divide the dough into two equal pieces. Working with one piece at a time, roll the dough on a lightly floured surface into an 8 by 15-inch rectangle. Cut the dough into twelve 4 by 2½-inch rectangles. Put the rectangles on the prepared sheet and lay another piece of parchment on top. Repeat with the remaining dough. Cover the sheet with plastic wrap and refrigerate the dough on the sheet until ready to use. Don't worry if the rectangles aren't perfect. Once the dough has rested you can roll and trim each piece to neaten them up if you'd like.

To prepare the filling, in a small saucepan, whisk together the sugar, cornstarch, nutmeg, cinnamon, and salt. Stir in the blackberries and peach and cook over medium heat until the fruit has broken down and the mixture has thickened, 6 to 8 minutes. Let cool completely.

Preheat the oven to 400°F. Line two baking sheets with parchment paper.

In a small bowl, make an egg wash by whisking together the egg yolk and the 2 teaspoons water. Lay out 6 dough rectangles on one of the prepared sheets. Dollop about 2 tablespoons of filling in the center of each rectangle. Brush the edges with some of the egg wash and top with another dough rectangle, pressing the edges with a fork to seal. With a paring knife, make a little slit in each pie to vent steam. Chill the assembled pies for 20 minutes.

Repeat with the remaining dough and filling on the other prepared baking sheet. Brush the tops of the chilled pies with egg wash. Bake until puffed and golden brown, 20 to 25 minutes. Repeat with the remaining pies. Let the pies cool slightly on a rack.

To prepare the glaze, whisk together the confectioners' sugar, cream cheese, and vanilla in a small bowl. Whisk in enough milk to make a thick glaze. Drizzle over the warm pies. Serve warm or at room temperature. These are really best the day they're made, but you can store leftovers in an airtight container at room temperature for up to 2 days. Glazed pies don't reheat well, but unglazed pies can be reheated in the oven on low heat.

INDONESIAN SPICED LAYER CAKE

SERVES 16

1¼ cups (2½ sticks)
unsalted butter,
at room temperature,
plus 3 tablespoons melted
butter, plus more for
greasing the pan

1½ cups (6¾ ounces)
all-purpose flour

1¼ teaspoons baking
powder

¾ teaspoon kosher salt

4 teaspoons freshly
grated nutmeg

1¾ teaspoons ground
cinnamon

¾ teaspoon freshly
ground cardamom

½ teaspoon ground cloves

1 cup granulated sugar

8 large eggs,
at room temperature,
separated

1 teaspoon pure
vanilla extract

Confectioners' sugar,
for dusting (optional)

Born from the marriage of rich Dutch butter cakes and luxurious spices, *kue lapis* is a traditional Indonesian favorite. Each thin layer is baked, one at a time, under the flame of a broiler, which gives the cake a lightly caramelized flavor and a gorgeous striped pattern. In the Netherlands, this cake is called *spekkoek* or "bacon cake" because the striped pattern is reminiscent of the beloved breakfast meat. Once the batter is assembled, the work goes quickly, but it's a job best undertaken in the wintertime, when the heat of the broiler feels lovely on a cold nose.

Preheat the broiler to high with the rack set in the center of the oven. (The "high" setting on my broiler is manageable, but if yours runs very hot, set the broiler to low. Your layers may take slightly longer to bake.) Butter an 8-inch square baking pan. Line the bottom of the pan with parchment paper and butter the parchment. In a small bowl, combine the flour, baking powder, and salt. In a medium bowl, combine the nutmeg, cinnamon, cardamom, and cloves.

In a large bowl, with an electric mixer, beat the butter and the sugar on medium speed until light and fluffy, 3 to 4 minutes. Beat in the egg yolks, 1 at a time, until blended and then beat in the vanilla.

In a large bowl, with clean beaters, beat the egg whites until medium-stiff, but not dry, peaks form, 2 to 4 minutes. Stir one-quarter of the egg whites into the butter-sugar mixture until smooth. The batter will be thick. With a rubber spatula, gently fold the remaining egg whites into the butter mixture. Then fold in the flour mixture. Add half of this batter to the bowl with the spice mixture and fold to combine.

Using an offset spatula, spread ½ cup of the spiced batter in the prepared pan. The layer will be thin. Broil until set and browned in spots, 30 seconds to 1 minute. Remove the pan from the oven, brush with some of the melted butter, and then carefully spread ½ cup of the plain batter over the baked layer. Broil until set, about 30 seconds to 1 minute. (You can touch the cake gently and feel if it is set and springy.) Repeat this process, layering, buttering, and broiling the two batters. As the cake gets higher in the pan and closer to the broiler, the layers may take less time to cook. Don't ever walk away from the broiler, and be sure to use a timer. The layers can burn in an instant. You should have about 10 layers in total.

Let the cake cool in the pan on a rack for about 15 minutes, then use a knife to loosen the edges and flip the cake out onto a serving plate. Remove the parchment. Serve warm or at room temperature, dusted with confectioners' sugar.

Store leftovers in an airtight container at room temperature for up to 2 days.

clove & cardamom

After my great-grandfather died, my great-grandmother dedicated herself to a few important things, including her family and her house. She was also in charge of maintaining the village shrine, just across the narrow, palm-tree-lined street from her home.

Shrines are all over Sri Lanka. Sometimes they are big and fancy, with golden pagodas and towering statues. Often they are more modest. My grandmother's shrine includes a white altar and a small statue of a seated Buddha with his hand extended, surrounded by neatly combed sand. It is decorated with Buddhist paper flags in blue, yellow, red, white, and orange, and always plenty of fresh flowers. Every day, my great-grandma made her way over to the little shrine to sweep the sand, clear the paths, and remove the old flowers.

The house where my great-grandparents lived still stands, and the shrine, still a popular spot in the village, is just as it was. We stop every time we pass it, as is the custom. I'm not a practicing Buddhist, but I do like to stop there and think of my great-grandmother. And I like to imagine her house across the street, just the way that my parents have always told me about it. The shiny green concrete floors, veined with darker green where the cracks were filled in. The windows, which had no panes, with their wooden shutters. The mahogany settee with the bright woven pillows. And the row of clove trees that stood sentry in the yard.

I love to hear about those clove trees. Thirty to forty feet tall, with shiny green leaves, the evergreen clove trees needed little tending but bore much fruit. My great-grandmother relied on the annual clove harvest as a part of her income. She leased each tree to an interested merchant. When the clusters of flower buds began to turn from pale green to bright red, the merchants would set up tents under their tree and live there until it was time to collect the clove buds—staking their claim to the trees to ward off thieves.

The trees provided bushels of valuable cloves and helped keep my great-grandmother in good financial standing until she died—at the ripe old age of 104. The clove trees afforded her the time to take care of that shrine.

Cardamom also grew here and there in my great-grandmother's yard, but it was never sold as cloves were. While cloves hang in the air like tiny chandeliers, cardamom grows along the ground. At the base of its leaves, along delicate stems, bloom tiny ruffled white flowers. These flowers produce the pods. My great-grandmother picked these pods only to use in the family cooking. I'll never understand this discrepancy in value—cardamom just might be my favorite spice of all. But the priorities that ruled in my great-grandmother's yard were also the priorities of the great spice empires.

CLOVES AND CARDAMOM IN HISTORY

Cloves and cardamom were both part of the ancient spice trade. Cardamom is native to the Western Ghat forests of the Malabar Coast of India. It grew alongside the Indian peppercorn from the same region, which was known as the "King of Spices," so cardamom was called "the Queen."

Arab traders were the first to bring cardamom from South Asia over to Babylon, Egypt, Greece, and Rome. We know that Arab traders kept the origin of cardamom a secret from the Mediterranean merchants, just as they did with their other precious commodities. But otherwise the early history of cardamom is difficult to trace. Historians aren't certain if the cardamom referenced in the early Greek texts is the cardamom we are familiar with today.

Once the Portuguese found the sea route to India, they exported cardamom along with ginger and black pepper. But it seems that cardamom didn't take off in Europe as quickly as the other spices. The historical importance of spices like cloves, cinnamon, and peppercorns is well documented, while cardamom rarely gets more than a passing mention.

I wonder if that had something to do with cultivation. For centuries, all of the world's cardamom grew wild. Actual cardamom plantations didn't exist until the British established them in India in the early 1800s. Perhaps because the plant required so little tending, it didn't lend itself to trade monopolies, and didn't attract the attention that other spices did.

The exceptions to this rule are the ninth-century Vikings, who discovered cardamom in the markets of Constantinople and brought it back to Scandinavia. I can't help but smile when I imagine burly Viking men falling helmet-over-beard in love with the sweet, eucalyptus-like aroma of cardamom, and dreaming of all the Nordic dishes, breads, and pastries that it would complement. Today Scandinavia is still among the world's top consumers of cardamom.

Cloves, on the other hand, were very rare. They initially grew only on five small, remote Indonesian islands in the Malay Archipelago called the Moluccas. The two most prominent of these islands, Ternate and Tidore, are also active volcanoes at least a mile high. The frequent eruptions were said to enrich the soil with nutrients and enhance the flavor of the spice. Ancient traders brought cloves from these tiny islands to Europe via the Indian Ocean, the Arabian Sea, and the grand bazaars of Alexandria, where they were sold as a luxury item.

Perhaps the remoteness of these islands explains the high value of cloves. Clearly the Dutch put a high price on them. By the time they controlled the spice trade in the seventeenth and eighteenth centuries, it was nearly impossible to grow cloves anywhere but the Moluccan Islands, as the Dutch made the export of seedlings from the islands a crime punishable by death. That certainly makes me wonder where my great-grandmother's Sri Lankan clove trees came from.

PIERRE POIVRE

I doubt cloves would have made it to my great-grandmother's land if it weren't for a French adventurer and amateur botanist named Pierre Poivre. Coincidentally, *poivre* is the French word for "pepper," but it was the trade in cloves and nutmeg that he changed forever.

By the eighteenth century, two hundred years after the Portuguese found a sea route to India, other spices, including peppercorn and cardamom, were making their way more easily around the world. That meant lower prices for the consumer—and smaller profits for the empires that had once been in control. Cloves and nutmeg were two of the spices that were still under strict Dutch control. Pierre Poivre was interested in trying to bring these lucrative plants into French hands.

Poivre became a political official on a French island outpost just east of Madagascar, what we today know as Mauritius, but was then called Île de France. On the grounds of his mansion, he collected one of the largest collections of tropical plants in the world. He worked to turn the island into a self-sufficient agricultural economy. His goal was to make Île de France and its island neighbor, Bourbon (today called Réunion), the two French territories in the Indian Ocean, spice islands. The way he accomplished this was both sneaky and ingenious.

In 1770, Poivre sent a battalion of men out to the Moluccas, and they hit the jackpot, thanks to an unimaginable stroke of luck. On the island of Ceram, the crew encountered a dissatisfied Dutchman who directed them to an island where natives were secretly growing cloves and nutmeg hidden from the Dutch. There they found hundreds of clove and nutmeg seedlings, and thousands of seeds and untreated nutmegs, which the Dutch were in the habit of covering with lime to render them infertile before exporting. Poivre's men were able to gather four hundred nutmeg trees and seventy clove trees to bring back to Île de France. Once they were distributed, the Dutch monopoly was over.

By the end of the eighteenth century, cloves had been successfully transplanted to Madagascar, Zanzibar, and Pemba, which are still great producers of the spice. Nutmeg went west to the Caribbean islands of Martinique and Grenada—still major producers. The English, who most likely stole cloves from the French West Indies, were able to transplant cloves to St. Kitts, also in the Caribbean. By then, cloves were also established in Sri Lanka. A little over a century later, my great-grandmother would be tending to her own trees.

WHAT ARE CLOVES?

Cloves, *Syzygium aromaticum*, are the unopened flower buds of a tall evergreen tree in the myrtle family. The rose-colored buds form in small clusters. Harvesters pick the buds before they open, anytime from December through April, depending on the region. After a few days of drying, the buds turn dark brown and begin to resemble the nails (*clous* in French) for which they were named. While they were originally native to the Maluku Islands (formerly known as the Moluccas) of present-day Indonesia, Zanzibar is now the world's leading producer of cloves.

BUYING AND STORING CLOVES

Buy whole cloves that are bright, reddish brown and leave a bit of oil when squeezed between your fingers. Darker cloves have been dried for too long and have less flavor. Whole cloves are easily ground in a spice grinder or using a mortar and pestle, but I find that dried ground cloves are perfectly acceptable. Unlike other spices, ground cloves retain their flavor over time. Stored in an airtight container in a cool, dry place, ground cloves will last up to a year or longer, and whole cloves should last at least that long.

WHAT IS CARDAMOM?

Native to India, green cardamom, *Elettaria cardamomum*, is the fruit of an herbaceous perennial bush of the ginger family. It grows up to 15 feet tall, with reedy stems and long green leaves. Just before they are fully ripe, the small, thin-skinned green fruit pods that grow at the base of the plant are cut off by hand and dried. Inside the pods are the dark brown seeds, which are crushed and ground for cooking. Until about two hundred years ago, when the British created the first cardamom plantations in India, all cardamom was harvested from wild plants. Today India and Guatemala are the world's largest producers.

White cardamom is simply bleached green cardamom. The flavor is mellow and somewhat bland. I don't recommend it.

Black cardamom, which is native to the Himalayas, is dried over wood fires, giving it a much more robust, smoky flavor better suited for savory preparations.

BUYING AND STORING CARDAMOM

For the freshest flavor, buy whole, unsplit green pods. They should be easy to find in the spice section of a well-stocked supermarket. Gently crush the pods to extract the flavorful seeds. The seeds can be ground in a spice grinder, or with a little elbow grease using a mortar and pestle. I go through cardamom fast, so I buy small bags of seeds that have been removed from the pod. That makes life easy! But removing the seeds from the pod also shortens their shelf life so you have to use them quickly. Ground cardamom is fine in a pinch, but the flavor of freshly ground is far superior. One teaspoon of ground cardamom equals about seven pods of the whole spice.

APRICOT-WALNUT GRANOLA BARS

MAKES ABOUT 12 BARS

¼ cup coconut oil, plus more for greasing the pan

2 cups (7 ounces) old-fashioned (rolled) oats

2¼ ounces (½ cup) walnuts, chopped

3 ounces (½ cup) dried whole apricots, chopped

½ cup (1½ ounces) unsweetened shredded coconut

¾ teaspoon freshly ground cardamom

½ teaspoon kosher salt

¼ cup Lyle's Golden Syrup or honey

¼ cup packed light brown sugar

2 tablespoons water

Store-bought granola bars are good in a pinch, but I take a distinct pleasure in making my own, exactly to my own specifications. I like mine best with unsweetened coconut, fleshy dried apricots, and plenty of cardamom. They have everything I want in a bar—tart, sweet, and spice. Feel free to use this recipe as a jumping-off point though: Swap in pecans, dried cherries, and cinnamon and you've got another story altogether. What about almonds? Or dried figs? Just keep the proportions of nuts, fruits, and spice the same as the recipe and you can have a great new bar for every day of the week.

Preheat the oven to 350°F. Lightly oil a 9-inch square baking pan and line with parchment paper, leaving a 2-inch overhang on two sides.

In a large bowl, combine the oats, walnuts, apricots, coconut, cardamom, and salt. Clip a candy thermometer to the side of a small saucepan and heat the syrup, brown sugar, and the water over medium-high heat. If the sugar mixture is too low, the temperature won't register properly on the thermometer. Tilt the pan so that the bulb of the thermometer is submerged in the syrup. Cook until the sugar reaches 248°F, 6 to 8 minutes. Remove the pot from the heat and whisk in the coconut oil. Add the syrup mixture to the oat mixture. Stir until everything is evenly coated.

Tip the mixture into the prepared baking pan and use a wet spatula to flatten it to an even thickness. You want to really push and compact the mixture as far as it will go.

Bake until set and deep golden brown, 25 to 30 minutes. It should smell nice and toasty. Let it cool completely in the pan on a rack. Using the parchment, lift the uncut bars out of the pan and onto a cutting board. Using a long, sharp knife, cut into bars. Wrap each of the bars in plastic wrap and store them in an airtight container at room temperature for up to 5 days or in the freezer for up to a month.

PISTACHIO AND CHOCOLATE BUTTER CAKE

SERVES 10

½ cup (1 stick) unsalted butter, at room temperature, plus more for greasing the pan

1¾ cups (7⅞ ounces) all-purpose flour

1¾ teaspoons baking powder

1 teaspoon freshly ground cardamom

½ teaspoon kosher salt

⅓ cup granulated sugar

2 large eggs, at room temperature

7 ounces (about ¾ cup) pistachio paste

½ cup whole milk, at room temperature

3 ounces chopped bittersweet chocolate (60 to 70 percent cacao) (about ¾ cup)

1¼ ounces (¼ cup) shelled raw pistachios, coarsely chopped

Confectioners' sugar, for sprinkling (optional)

Pistachio paste is simply pistachio nuts ground with sugar to a smooth, spreadable paste. Look for it in the baking aisle of a well-stocked supermarket, online, or in a European specialty grocery store. It's the key to getting the crumb of this tea cake perfect—the paste adds just the right amount of moisture to the batter. Use it here or in the lacy Crêpe Cake with Pistachio Cream (page 161), and be sure to keep the leftovers for spreading thick on a slice of toast.

Preheat the oven to 350°F. Butter a 9-inch springform pan.

In a medium bowl, whisk together the flour, baking powder, cardamom, and salt. In a large bowl, with an electric mixer, beat the butter and sugar on medium speed until pale and fluffy, 3 to 4 minutes. Add the eggs, one at a time, and then beat in the pistachio paste. Add the flour mixture and the milk alternately, in three additions, beating a bit between each, beginning and ending with the flour mixture. Fold in the chocolate.

Pour the batter into the prepared pan and smooth the top. Sprinkle the top with the pistachios. Bake until golden brown around the edges and a toothpick inserted into the center comes out with moist crumbs attached, 30 to 40 minutes. Let cool in the pan on a wire rack for 10 minutes. Cut around the edges and then release the sides of the pan from the cake and let it cool completely. Dust with confectioners' sugar to serve.

Store the cake, well wrapped, at room temperature for up to 3 days or frozen for up to a month.

INSIDE-OUT FRUITCAKE

SERVES 10

TOPPING

¾ cup water

6 ounces (1 cup) dried whole tart cherries

6 ounces (1 cup) dried whole apricots

¼ cup (½ stick) unsalted butter

¼ cup packed dark brown sugar

2¼ ounces (½ cup) walnuts, coarsely chopped

CAKE

1½ cups (6¾ ounces) all-purpose flour

1½ teaspoons baking powder

½ teaspoon ground cinnamon

½ teaspoon ground cloves

¾ teaspoon kosher salt

½ cup (1 stick) unsalted butter, at room temperature

⅔ cup packed dark brown sugar

2 large eggs plus 1 large egg yolk

2 teaspoons pure vanilla extract

¾ cup buttermilk

TO FINISH

1 tablespoon dark rum (optional)

Every culture seems to have its own version of fruitcake. Whether it's laden with alcohol, Technicolor-candied fruit, or rich almond paste, it always comes loaded with history. Early Egyptians left fruitcakes in the tombs of their loved ones. Roman soldiers were known to bring it into battle.

My version turns fruitcake inside out and upside down. Rather than hide the fruit inside, I show it off. And what starts out as the bottom becomes the top. First, sweet and salty caramel, plump dried fruit, and nuts are topped with a delicately spiced buttermilk batter. Once baked, flipped, and splashed with rum, the alcohol, the fruit, and the warmth of the cloves work in harmony to create something more than the sum of the parts. I love the sweet-tart combination of apricots and tart cherries, but you can use any dried fruit you like.

Preheat the oven to 350°F.

To prepare the topping, bring the water to a boil over medium-high heat in a 10-inch ovenproof skillet. Add the cherries and apricots. Decrease the heat to medium and simmer, stirring, until the fruit is just beginning to soften, about 2 minutes. Remove from the heat, cover, and set aside until the fruit is plump, about 10 minutes. Pour the fruit and any remaining liquid into a medium bowl.

To prepare the cake, whisk together the flour, baking powder, cinnamon, cloves, and salt in a medium bowl. In a large bowl, beat the ½ cup of butter and the ⅔ cup of brown sugar with an electric mixer on medium speed until pale and fluffy, 3 to 4 minutes. Beat in eggs and yolk, one at a time, until combined, and then stir in the vanilla. With the mixer on low, alternate adding the flour mixture and buttermilk to the butter mixture, starting with the flour. Set the batter aside while you finish the topping.

CONTINUED

To finish the topping, return the skillet to the heat and melt the ¼ cup butter over medium heat. Add the ¼ cup brown sugar, stirring constantly, until the mixture bubbles and starts to take on the texture of caramel, about 2 minutes. Remove from the heat and arrange the walnuts and the fruit (along with any liquid) evenly in the skillet.

Pour the batter over the fruit in the skillet, and smooth the top. Bake, rotating the skillet halfway through, until golden brown and a toothpick inserted in the center comes out with moist crumbs attached, 28 to 32 minutes. Let the cake cool in the skillet on a rack for 5 minutes. Run a knife around the edge of the skillet and carefully invert the cake onto a serving plate. Scrape any caramel or fruit from the pan onto the cake. Drizzle with rum. Serve warm or at room temperature.

The cake is best the day it's made. Store leftovers, well wrapped, at room temperature, for up to 2 days.

MANGO POPS

MAKES 10 POPS

3 to 4 large mangoes (9 to 10 ounces each), preferably Champagne

¼ cup Lyle's Golden Syrup

¾ teaspoon freshly ground cardamom

½ cup plain whole milk yogurt

½ cup heavy cream

Pinch of kosher salt

I've always known my grandmother's sister Kusum as "Mango Pop Auntie." She used to bring her namesake treats with her on visits, handing them out to my brother and me whenever we began to overheat in the Sri Lankan sun. Ice-cold and juicy, they were refreshing beyond belief.

My version of her signature pop includes a hit of cardamom and a bit of dairy. The tang of the yogurt mellows out the sweetness of the mango in a most addictive way. These pops are really best with the flesh of fresh, perfectly ripe peeled mangoes, blended to a very smooth puree with a high-speed blender. I prefer Champagne mangoes for their complex flavor but any variety will do. Don't be tempted to use frozen mangoes for this dessert. They never blend as smooth as fresh fruit.

Have ready ten 3-ounce ice-pop molds and sticks.

Peel each mango and cut the flesh off the pit. Chop the flesh and add to a blender. Puree until very smooth. Reserve 2 cups for the pops. Save any extra for your next cocktail party or to top a stack of Sunday morning pancakes.

In a 4-cup liquid measuring cup, whisk together the mango puree, syrup, and cardamom. Stir in the yogurt, heavy cream, and salt.

Fill the ice pop molds, cover, add sticks, and freeze until solid, at least 12 hours. To release the pops, run the bottom of the mold under warm water very briefly. Serve right away or store individually in small, resealable plastic bags for up to 2 weeks.

ORANGE-CLOVE PULL-APART BREAD

MAKES 1 LOAF

DOUGH

¼ cup (½ stick) unsalted butter, cut into pieces, plus more for greasing the bowl and the pan

½ cup whole milk

1 large egg, lightly beaten

1 tablespoon pure vanilla extract

1 cup (4½ ounces) all-purpose flour

1 cup (4½ ounces) bread flour

¼ cup sugar

1½ teaspoons active dry yeast

½ teaspoon kosher salt

⅛ teaspoon ground cloves

FILLING

⅓ cup sugar

2 tablespoons finely grated orange zest (from 2 oranges)

¼ teaspoon kosher salt

3 tablespoons unsalted butter, at room temperature

When a piping-hot loaf of bread comes out of the oven, all I want to do is tear into it with my hands (maybe even teeth). Forget about waiting for it to cool or grabbing a knife. Usually, my civilized side keeps me in check. Usually. But the great thing about this loaf is that there's no need to hold back. The dough is cut into squares so that it bakes up into already portioned slices, each steeped in butter and orange zest, spiced with ground clove, and ready to be ripped apart while still warm. Follow your animal instincts. Bake this bread.

Lightly butter a large bowl and set aside.

To prepare the dough, bring the milk just to a boil over medium heat in a small pot. Watch closely to ensure that it doesn't boil over. Remove from the heat and add butter to the pot to melt. Put the mixture in a small bowl and let it cool to 105°F to 110°F. (It should be warm to the touch but not too hot.) Add the egg and vanilla and stir to combine.

In the bowl of a stand mixer fitted with the paddle attachment, or in a large bowl with a wooden spoon, combine the all-purpose flour, bread flour, sugar, yeast, salt, and cloves on low speed. Add the milk mixture and mix just until combined.

Switch to the dough hook and knead the dough on low speed until smooth and elastic, about 6 minutes. Or, tip the dough onto a work surface and knead by hand for about 12 minutes. You shouldn't need to add flour. Form the dough into a ball, place the ball in the prepared bowl, and cover with plastic wrap. Leave it in a warm, draft-free spot until it has doubled in size. This could take anywhere between 30 minutes and 2 hours. It all depends on how warm your house is.

CONTINUED

Meanwhile prepare the filling. In a small bowl, mix together the sugar, orange zest, and salt. Stir in the butter to make a paste. Cover with plastic wrap and set aside.

Butter a 4½ by 8½-inch loaf pan and line with parchment paper, leaving a 2-inch overhang on the two long sides. Butter the parchment.

When the dough has doubled, tip it out onto a very lightly floured work surface. Knead it once or twice to expel the air and then roll it into a 9-inch square. Spread the filling evenly over the surface. Cut the square into 4 equal strips. Stack the strips on top of each other, filling side up. Cut the stack to make 4 piles of 4 squares each. Set each stack, on its side like dominoes, in the loaf pan. Cover loosely with plastic wrap, and let the dough rest until it has risen to just under the lip of the loaf pan, about 1 hour.

Preheat the oven to 375°F.

Uncover the loaf and bake until golden brown and puffed, 30 to 35 minutes. Cover the loaf with aluminum foil if it is browning too quickly. To see if it's ready, give the center slice a wiggle—if it's set in place, the loaf is ready to come out. If the middle of that center slice seems soft, give it another few minutes. Let cool on a rack for 15 minutes then, using the parchment, lift the loaf out and onto a serving plate. Slip out the parchment before serving.

The bread is best eaten warm the day it's made. Store leftovers, well wrapped, at room temperature, and reheat, wrapped in foil, in a low oven.

BUTTERY SHORTBREAD WITH COFFEE AND CARDAMOM

MAKES 16 COOKIES

¾ cup (1½ sticks) unsalted butter, at room temperature but not too soft, plus more for greasing the pan

2 teaspoons ground coffee (a light or medium roast is best)

1 teaspoon cardamom seeds, from 20 pods (or 2 teaspoons freshly ground)

1¼ cups (5⅝ ounces) all-purpose flour

⅓ cup confectioners' sugar

¼ cup packed dark brown sugar

½ teaspoon kosher salt

1 teaspoon pure vanilla extract

Shortbread is as easy as it gets. Just mix up the dough, pop it into the pan, chill, and bake. I love the simplicity. Coffee and cardamom is a classic Eastern flavor pairing and a tasty one at that. The sweet, aromatic spice and the bitter beans go hand in hand. For this recipe, I like to use whatever ground coffee I have on hand for my morning cup. Give it an extra whiz in a spice grinder to make it extra fine so it distributes nicely throughout the dough.

Preheat the oven to 325°F. Butter a 9-inch fluted tart pan with a removable bottom or a 9-inch springform pan.

Using a coffee or spice grinder, process the coffee and cardamom until very finely ground. In a large bowl, whisk together the coffee mixture, flour, confectioners' sugar, brown sugar, and salt. Add the butter and vanilla and beat with an electric mixer on medium speed just until moist crumbs form and the butter is evenly dispersed, about 1 minute.

Tip the dough into the prepared pan and use your fingers to press it into an even layer on the bottom. If the dough has gotten too soft, you can use an offset spatula to spread it evenly. Freeze until firm, about 15 minutes.

Bake the frozen shortbread in the pan on a rimmed baking sheet (to catch any butter that might ooze out) until the dough is no longer wet and the top is golden brown, 40 to 45 minutes. Immediately, and while the dough is still warm, use a sharp paring knife to cut it into 16 thin wedges, then set it on a rack to cool completely. When it's cool, remove the pan edge, run a thin knife or a spatula between the cookies and the pan bottom, and gently break the cookies apart.

Store the shortbread in an airtight container at room temperature for up to 5 days or in the freezer for up to a month.

ORANGE AND HONEY BAKLAVA

MAKES ABOUT 25 PIECES

½ cup (1 stick) unsalted butter, melted, plus more for greasing the pan

1 orange

⅔ cup plus 2 tablespoons sugar

5 tablespoons water

1 teaspoon honey

1 teaspoon rose water

5 ounces (1 cup) shelled raw pistachios

5 ounces (1 cup) blanched almonds

1 teaspoon cardamom seeds, from 20 pods (or 2 teaspoons freshly ground)

½ teaspoon kosher salt

14 sheets prepared phyllo dough, thawed if frozen

Traditional baklava can be wonderful, but too often it's so laden with drippy sugar syrup that the delicate flavors of the ingredients are lost. Those tastes are too good to miss! I've spruced up my baklava with the essence of honey, orange, and rose water, and soaked it in just enough fragrant syrup to hold it together and accentuate the beauty of all the parts. Without too much syrup, the buttery phyllo emerges both crisp and chewy.

Don't be intimidated by phyllo dough. As long as you keep the sheets covered while you work, to keep them moist enough to work with, not much can go wrong. Little tears disappear once the dish is layered together.

Butter a 9-inch square baking pan and line with parchment paper, leaving a 2-inch overhang on two sides. Butter the parchment.

Finely grate 2 teaspoons of zest from the orange and set aside. Then squeeze 2 teaspoons of juice.

In a small saucepan, bring ⅔ cup of the sugar and the water to a simmer over medium heat and cook until the sugar is dissolved, about 2 minutes. Let cool completely then stir in the honey, rose water, and orange juice.

In a food processor fitted with the metal blade, pulse the pistachios, almonds, cardamom, salt, orange zest, and the remaining 2 tablespoons sugar until the nuts are very finely ground. (They must be very finely ground for the baklava layers to stay together.)

Unroll the stack of phyllo on a work surface and trim it to a 9-inch square. Immediately cover the stack with a layer of plastic wrap and a dish towel to keep the plastic in place. Keep the phyllo covered while you work, lifting the plastic and towel only to grab one sheet at a time. Lay 1 sheet of phyllo on the bottom of the prepared pan. Brush the sheet lightly with butter and add another sheet. Repeat this process with 3 more sheets. Top evenly with half of the nut mixture and drizzle with 1 tablespoon butter. Add 4 more sheets of phyllo, each brushed with butter. Top with the remaining nut mixture and another tablespoon of butter. Finish with the remaining 5 sheets of phyllo, each one brushed with butter.

Using a sharp knife, make 5 parallel cuts through the baklava at a 45-degree angle. Then, turning the knife about 90 degrees in the opposite direction, make five more. Be careful not to cut the parchment on the bottom. Bake until golden brown and crisp, 30 to 35 minutes. Pour the cool syrup all over the warm baklava.

Let cool completely at room temperature, then cover with plastic wrap and let stand overnight. Using the parchment, lift the baklava out of the pan and onto a cutting board and recut the pieces to serve.

Store the baklava in an airtight container at room temperature for up to 5 days.

SOUR CHERRY CHEESECAKE BARS

MAKES 16 BARS

COMPOTE
3 cups (15 ounces)
pitted sour cherries,
thawed if frozen

⅓ cup sugar

¼ teaspoon ground cloves

¼ teaspoon ground
cinnamon

Pinch of kosher salt

1 tablespoon cornstarch

PASTRY
2 cups (9 ounces)
all-purpose flour

⅓ cup sugar

2 teaspoons baking powder

½ teaspoon salt

¾ cup (1½ sticks)
cold unsalted butter,
cut into cubes

3 large egg yolks

CHEESECAKE
8 ounces cream cheese,
at room temperature

¼ cup sugar

1 large egg

Sour cherries are gorgeous. Their bright red skin practically sparkles. But just like the rubies they resemble, they can be hard to come by. Look for them at your local farmers' market in the heat of summer. The good news is that they freeze well. I always buy pints and pints of them when they appear and set them aside for making pies, cobblers, and bars all year round. To store sour cherries, pit them first, then freeze them in a single layer on a parchment-lined, rimmed baking sheet. Then store the frozen berries in an airtight container. They should last for up to a year.

These cheesecake bars are an excellent vessel for summer sour cherries. Making the spiced compote from scratch, instead of using store-bought jam, makes the fruit, and not the sugar, the star. I brought these to my accountant when he was doing my taxes, and he knocked one hundred dollars off his fee.

Preheat the oven to 350°F. Line a 9-inch square baking pan with parchment paper, leaving a 2-inch overhang on two sides.

To prepare the compote, bring the cherries, sugar, cloves, cinnamon, and salt to a simmer in a small saucepan over medium heat. Cook until the cherries are very tender, about 5 minutes, then crush them in the pan with a potato masher. In a small bowl, whisk together the cornstarch and about 2 tablespoons of the juice from the cherry mixture. Add the cornstarch mixture back into the saucepan and simmer until thickened, 2 to 3 minutes. Remove from the heat and let the compote cool slightly. It should be the consistency of a loose jam. Reserve 1½ cups of the compote for the bars. (If you have a little extra compote, save it for a scoop of vanilla ice cream.)

To prepare the pastry, in the bowl of a food processor fitted with the metal blade, add the flour, sugar, baking powder, and salt and pulse to combine. Add the butter and pulse

CONTINUED

until the mixture resembles coarse meal. Add the egg yolks and pulse just until the mixture is evenly moistened but still somewhat sandy. Sprinkle a little bit more than half of the flour mixture in the prepared pan and press it down into an even layer. Bake until set and golden brown, 20 to 25 minutes. Let cool slightly.

To prepare the cheesecake layer, whisk together the cream cheese and sugar in a medium bowl until smooth. Whisk in the egg.

Spread the cream cheese mixture evenly over the baked bottom crust. Drop the cherry compote in dollops evenly on top of the cream cheese mixture and then gently spread it out, keeping the cream cheese layer in place as best you can. Sprinkle the remaining flour mixture on top, squeezing it to make some clumps bigger than the others.

Bake until the cheesecake layer is set and the topping is deep golden brown, 30 to 40 minutes. Let cool completely on a rack. To serve, cut around the edges to loosen them from the pan, then use the parchment to lift the uncut bars out of the pan and onto a cutting board. Use a long sharp knife to cut into bars.

Store the bars in an airtight container in the refrigerator for up to 3 days.

BROWN SUGAR MERINGUE COOKIES

MAKES ABOUT 2 DOZEN COOKIES

¼ cup confectioners' sugar

¼ cup packed dark brown sugar

1 tablespoon cornstarch

¼ teaspoon kosher salt

¼ teaspoon cream of tartar

3 large egg whites, at room temperature

½ teaspoon freshly ground cardamom

2¼ ounces bittersweet chocolate (60 to 70 percent cacao), finely chopped (about ½ cup)

2¼ ounces (½ cup) walnuts, finely chopped

I'm always making custard, every chance I get. So I love recipes that use up the egg whites that I inevitably have in my fridge. These meringue cookies will surprise you. They're not nearly as sweet as you expect: instead, they have a toasted sugar flavor punctuated by bittersweet walnuts, oozing melted chocolate, and aromatic cardamom.

Timing is everything here. I like to pull these cookies out right when the outside feels crisp and the center holds just a touch of chew. They will harden a bit more as they cool. But if you happen to bake them a minute or two too long, don't worry. They'll just be completely crisp, and that's delicious too!

Preheat the oven to 300°F. Line two baking sheets with parchment paper.

In a large bowl, whisk together the confectioners' sugar, brown sugar, cornstarch, salt, and cream of tartar. Add the egg whites and whisk to combine.

Set the bowl over a saucepan of barely simmering water. Make sure the bottom of the bowl isn't touching the water. Whisk the egg mixture until warm, thick, and foamy and all of the sugar has dissolved, about 3 minutes. (Rub a little bit of the mixture between your fingertips to check.) Remove from the heat and beat with an electric mixer on high speed until the mixture makes glossy, stiff peaks, about 3 minutes. Gently fold in the cardamom, chocolate, and walnuts.

Drop the mixture in 1½-tablespoon scoops onto the prepared sheets at least ½ inch apart. Bake the meringues until the outside is crisp, 45 to 50 minutes, rotating the sheets halfway through. Slip the parchment paper onto racks to cool completely, then peel the cookies from the parchment.

Store the cookies in an airtight container at room temperature for up to 5 days.

CARDAMOM CREAM–FILLED SUGAR DOUGHNUTS

MAKES ABOUT 1 DOZEN DOUGHNUTS

DOUGH
¾ cup whole milk

2 large eggs plus 2 large egg yolks, lightly beaten

6 tablespoons (¾ stick) unsalted butter, at room temperature, cut into pieces, plus more for greasing the bowl

3½ cups (15¾ ounces) all-purpose flour, plus ½ cup if necessary and more for the work surface and the parchment

¼ cup sugar

1 tablespoon active dry yeast

1 teaspoon kosher salt

CREAM
2½ cups whole milk

2 tablespoons green cardamom pods, lightly crushed

4 large egg yolks

¼ cup cornstarch

¼ cup sugar

½ teaspoon kosher salt

⅓ cup heavy cream

TO FINISH
Vegetable oil, for frying

¾ cup sugar

The sight of cardamom takes me right back to the Engineer's Bungalow, as my grandparents' house was affectionately known in the village where they lived. The little pods were used to flavor the neon-yellow turmeric rice that we ate on every special occasion. As a little kid, I hated that rice and quickly grew frustrated picking the curry leaves and cardamom husks out of my dinner. Now I think cardamom is my favorite of all the spices. I would put it in everything if I could. And what I would do for some of that special-occasion rice!

Cardamom mixed with cream is one of the loveliest things on the planet. It's no wonder so many South Asian desserts highlight this classic combination. Cardamom cream nestled in a fluffy doughnut makes a surprising and wonderful alternative to classic cream doughnuts—think Bombay Cream instead of Boston Cream.

To prepare the dough, bring the milk just to a boil over medium heat in a small pot. Watch closely to ensure that the milk doesn't boil over. Pour the milk into a measuring cup and top it off with enough water to bring the level back to ¾ cup. Let it cool to between 105°F and 110°F. (It should be warm to the touch but not too hot.) Add the eggs and egg yolks to the warm milk mixture and whisk gently to combine.

Butter a medium bowl and set aside.

In the bowl of a stand mixer fitted with the paddle attachment, or in a large bowl with a wooden spoon, combine the flour, sugar, yeast, and salt. Add the milk mixture and mix just until combined. Switch to the dough hook and knead the dough on low speed, about 3 minutes. Or, tip the dough out onto a lightly floured surface and knead by hand for about 6 minutes. At this point, you could add a bit more flour, if necessary, but resist the urge to add too much. The dough should be workable but still somewhat sticky.

CONTINUED

Add the butter, a piece or two at a time. It may look like it's not getting in there but don't worry, it will; just keep adding and kneading. (You might have to stop the mixer and knead the butter in with your hands for a minute to get it started.) Once the butter is incorporated, increase the speed to medium and knead the dough for another few minutes until the dough is smooth and elastic. Or tip the dough onto a very lightly floured work surface and knead by hand until smooth. Put the dough in the prepared bowl, cover with plastic wrap, and refrigerate for at least 3 hours (and up to 12 hours).

Meanwhile, prepare the cardamom cream. Set a fine-mesh sieve over a medium bowl. In a medium saucepan, bring the milk and cardamom to a simmer over medium heat. Remove from the heat and set aside to infuse for 10 minutes. In a large bowl, whisk together the egg yolks, cornstarch, sugar, and salt. Add the warm milk mixture to the yolk mixture and whisk to combine. Pour the mixture back into the saucepan, bring to a boil over medium heat, stirring constantly, and cook until the mixture is thick, 3 to 6 minutes. Strain the mixture through the sieve into the bowl, discarding any solids. Press plastic wrap onto the surface of the cream and refrigerate until cooled completely.

Line two baking sheets with parchment paper. Dust the paper well with flour.

Tip the cold dough onto a lightly floured work surface and roll it into a 9½ by 12½-inch rectangle. It should be about ½ inch thick. Using a 3-inch round cookie cutter, cut out 12 dough rounds and set them on the prepared sheets. Lightly cover them with plastic wrap and set in a warm place to proof. This could take 30 minutes or 2 hours, depending on how warm your house is and how cold the dough was. It's best to keep an eye on the dough rather than the clock. The dough should look puffy and spring back slowly when pressed gently.

When you're ready to fry, line a rimmed baking sheet (or a few plates) with paper towels. Put the sugar in a medium bowl. Add the oil to a medium, heavy-bottomed pot. You should have about 2 inches of oil. Attach a candy thermometer to the side of the pot and heat the oil to between 350°F and 360°F. Carefully add 2 to 3 doughnuts to the oil and fry them until golden brown, 2 to 3 minutes per side. Using a slotted spoon, put the doughnuts on the paper towels. After about 1 minute, when the doughnuts are cool enough to handle, toss them in sugar. Repeat with the remaining dough.

To fill the doughnuts, using the handle of a wooden spoon or a chopstick, poke a hole into one side of each doughnut. Be careful not to poke through the other side. Whisk the heavy cream to stiff peaks. Whisk the chilled cardamom cream to loosen it, then fold in the whipped cream. Spoon the cream mixture into a pastry bag fitted with a small round tip. For each doughnut, insert the tip of the pastry bag into the hole and gently squeeze to fill.

Serve immediately. Doughnuts are outstanding the day they're made.

DATE NUT COOKIE PIES

MAKES ABOUT 3½ DOZEN COOKIES

PASTRY

3 cups (13½ ounces) all-purpose flour, plus more for the work surface

¾ cup confectioners' sugar

¾ teaspoon kosher salt

1 cup plus 2 tablespoons (2¼ sticks) unsalted butter, cut into cubes

3 large egg yolks

4 to 6 tablespoons heavy cream, plus more for brushing

Sanding sugar, for sprinkling (optional)

FILLING

3¼ ounces (¾ cup) chopped pitted Medjool dates

¾ cup water

1 ounce (¼ cup) pecans

1 ounce (¼ cup) walnuts

2 tablespoons honey or sugar

1 tablespoon finely grated orange zest (from 1 orange)

1 teaspoon freshly ground cardamom

¼ teaspoon ground cloves

¼ teaspoon kosher salt

Don't let the humble name fool you. These little cookies are bursting with flavor. They're reminiscent of those fig cookies you had as a kid—raised to the third power. The cream pastry is tender and flaky, and the honey-kissed filling, just sweet enough, is deepened by plump Medjool dates. They're also bite-size and adorable.

To prepare the pastry, combine the flour, confectioners' sugar, and salt in the bowl of a food processor fitted with the metal blade. Add the butter and pulse until the mixture resembles coarse meal. Add the egg yolks and 3 tablespoons of the cream and pulse just until the dough starts to come together. Add more cream if necessary but stop before the dough is too wet. Tip half of the dough out onto a piece of plastic wrap and form it into a disk. Repeat with the remaining dough. Chill the disks for at least 2 hours.

To prepare the filling, bring the dates and the water to a simmer over medium heat in a small saucepan. Cook until the dates are very soft, about 5 minutes. Transfer the dates and the water to the bowl of a food processor fitted with the metal blade and add the pecans, walnuts, honey, orange zest, cardamom, cloves, and salt and pulse until you have a chunky paste. Let cool completely.

Line two baking sheets with parchment paper.

Working with one disk at a time, roll the dough out to a thickness of ⅛ inch on a very lightly floured surface. (Less flour means a more tender cookie.) Using a 2-inch cookie cutter, cut out circles of dough and set them about 1 inch apart on the prepared baking sheet. Repeat with the remaining disk. You can reroll the dough once if you like.

Scoop about a rounded ½ teaspoon of filling onto half of the dough circles. Brush the edges of the filling-topped circles with a bit of cream and top with another dough circle, gently pressing the edges to seal. Once you've sandwiched all of the cookies, use a fork to crimp all of the edges.

Chill the cookies until firm, about 30 minutes. Preheat the oven to 350°F.

Brush the top of each cookie with cream and sprinkle with a bit of sanding sugar. Bake until the cookies are golden and crisp, 25 to 30 minutes, rotating the sheets halfway through. Let the cookies cool completely on a rack.

Store the cookies in an airtight container at room temperature for up to 5 days.

PEAR AND CHOCOLATE PAN CHARLOTTE

SERVES 8

10 tablespoons (1¼ sticks) unsalted butter, at room temperature

2 to 4 tablespoons packed dark brown sugar, depending on the sweetness of the pears

¼ teaspoon ground cloves

¼ teaspoon kosher salt

2½ pounds (about 5 medium) ripe Bartlett or D'Anjou pears, peeled, cored, and chopped

8 to 10 slices brioche, cut ½ inch thick

3 ounces bittersweet chocolate (60 to 70 percent cacao), chopped (about ⅔ cup)

Confectioners' sugar, for serving

A traditional charlotte is made in a special steel mold with handles and flared sides. The pan is lined with sliced bread or ladyfingers, filled with mousse or compote, topped off with more bread or cookies, and baked or set in the fridge. My simplified version uses just one skillet and comes together with far less fuss. The result is much more rustic and homey than the classic European beauty, but equally delicious—and maybe even more so, because in a skillet, the fruit and bread caramelize beautifully. This charlotte makes a stellar weekend breakfast or a comforting dessert dusted with confectioners' sugar.

Preheat the oven to 375°F.

In a 12-inch ovenproof skillet, melt ¼ cup of the butter over medium-high heat. Add the sugar, cloves, and salt and stir to combine. Add the pears, bring to a simmer, and cook, stirring occasionally, until the pears have broken down and the mixture is lightly caramelized, 10 to 15 minutes. Adjust the heat as necessary to keep the pears from scorching. Pour the pear mixture onto a plate to cool, and clean the skillet.

Spread the remaining butter evenly on both sides of each slice of bread. Line the bottom of the skillet with half of the bread, overlapping the slices as necessary. Sprinkle the chocolate evenly over the bread layer, then top with the pear mixture. Top with the remaining bread, arranged in a pretty pattern.

Bake until the bread is golden brown and the pears are very hot, 40 to 50 minutes. Cover the pan with aluminum foil if the bread is getting too brown. Let cool slightly then dust with confectioners' sugar and serve warm.

SEMLOR (SWEDISH CREAM BUNS)

MAKES 12 BUNS

DOUGH

6 tablespoons (¾ stick)
unsalted butter, plus more
for greasing the bowl

1 cup whole milk

½ cup granulated sugar

2½ teaspoons active
dry yeast

1 large egg, lightly beaten

3 cups (13½ ounces)
all-purpose flour,
plus more if needed
and for the work surface

1 teaspoon crushed
cardamom seeds

1 teaspoon kosher salt

1 large egg yolk

2 teaspoons water

FILLING

14 ounces (1½ cups)
almond paste

½ cup whole milk

TO FINISH

1½ cups heavy cream

1 to 2 tablespoons
confectioners' sugar,
plus more for sprinkling

A *semla*, the singular of *semlor*, is a perfect Swedish treat:
a soft, cardamom-scented roll filled with creamy almond
paste and billowy whipped cream. Simple. Satisfying.
Delicious. I taste-tested my way through quite a few on
a recent trip to Sweden. Believe me, these beauties are
worth trying.

There are a few ways to eat a semla. Some people like to
keep their hands clean and dig in with a fork. Some eat the
lid first, making the bottom half easier to manage by hand.
I like to grab the whole thing like a sandwich, try to unhinge
my jaw, and take impossibly large bites—the inevitable
result is cream up my nose. But the most traditional way
is called *hetvägg,* which means "hot wall" in Swedish. For
hetvägg, the semla is set in a bowl of warm milk and eaten
with a spoon. If that's not the coziest thing imaginable,
I don't know what is.

Lightly butter a large bowl.

To prepare the dough, bring the milk just to a boil over
medium heat in a small pot. Watch closely to ensure that
the milk doesn't boil over. Remove from the heat and
add the butter to the pot to melt. Put the mixture in the
bowl of a stand mixer or a large bowl and let it cool to 105°F
to 110°F. (It should be warm to the touch but not too hot.)

With the mixer fitted with the paddle attachment, or with
a wooden spoon, add the sugar, yeast, and whole egg to the
milk mixture. Add the flour, cardamom, and salt and mix
to combine.

Switch to the dough hook and knead the dough on low
speed until smooth and elastic, about 6 minutes. Or, tip
the dough onto a lightly floured work surface and knead
by hand for about 12 minutes. Add 1 to 2 tablespoons more
flour, a little at a time if necessary. But resist the urge to
add too much. The dough should still be a little sticky.

CONTINUED

Form the dough into a ball, place it in the prepared bowl, and cover with plastic wrap. Leave it in a warm, draft-free spot until it has doubled in size. This could take 30 minutes or 2 hours depending on the temperature. Keep an eye on the dough rather than the clock.

Line two baking sheets with parchment paper.

Turn the dough out onto a very lightly floured surface and knead it a few times. Divide the dough into 12 equal pieces. Flatten each ball slightly and fold in thirds, like a letter. Then turn each piece over and shape it into a ball. Roll each piece by forming a claw with your hand around the dough ball and moving it in a circle. Making a neat, tight ball is important to give the finished rolls a nice shape. Divide the balls between the prepared baking sheets. Cover lightly with plastic wrap. Place the sheets in a warm spot until the balls have doubled in size, about 1 hour.

Preheat the oven to 375°F.

In a small bowl, whisk together the egg yolk and the water. Lightly brush the tops and sides of the balls with the egg mixture. Bake until golden brown, 18 to 20 minutes. Let the rolls cool completely on a rack.

Once the rolls are completely cool, use a serrated knife to cut off the top third of each bun. Pull out some of the center of each bun to make room for the filling. (This makes a tasty snack for the baker or a nice addition to the topping of a fruit crisp.)

To prepare the filling, process the almond paste with the milk until smooth in a food processor fitted with the metal blade.

To assemble the buns, whip the cream and confectioners' sugar to soft peaks. Fill each bun with 2 tablespoons of the almond filling and a generous scoop of whipped cream. Top with the bun lids and sprinkle with confectioners' sugar.

The finished semlor are best the day they're made, but you can make the rolls in advance and freeze them for another day.

MAPLE-POACHED QUINCE

SERVES 6

½ cup maple syrup

6 green cardamom pods, lightly crushed

Pinch of kosher salt

2 cups water

2 medium quince (about 9 ounces each), peeled and cut into 8 wedges

Poached quince is simple perfection. During poaching, the hard pale flesh takes on a lovely rosy pink color and becomes soft and creamy. Let the fruit cool a bit and slice the wedges over ice cream or yogurt, drizzled with the poaching liquid, or serve the fruit alongside a favorite cheese or on top of a slice of pound cake.

Keep an eye on the liquid level as the fruit poaches. If it takes longer than an hour, you may need to add a bit more water to keep the fruit submerged.

In a medium saucepan, combine the maple syrup, cardamom pods, salt, and water.

Place one quince wedge, flat side down, on a cutting board and, using a sharp knife, cut a V-shape in the center to remove the seeds. Repeat with the remaining wedges, transferring the prepared quince to the saucepan as you go.

Cut a circle of parchment that is about 1 inch larger than the circumference of your saucepan. Cut a small hole in the center of the circle. Bring the mixture to a simmer on medium-high heat, then decrease the heat to a very gentle simmer. Place the parchment directly on top of the fruit in the liquid. Cook until the quince is tender when pierced with a knife, flipping the wedges occasionally, 50 to 60 minutes, but it could take longer depending on the quince. Keep an eye on the pot and add more water if necessary to keep the fruit submerged. Let the fruit cool completely in the syrup.

To serve, cut the cooled fruit into thick slices and drizzle with the syrup. Store the quince in an airtight container submerged in the syrup for up to 1 week.

CHAPTER 5
vanilla

My dad's father was born in 1910 in Kandy, Sri Lanka, and that's more or less where he stayed. He became the manager of several coconut plantations across the Kurunegala district, about 25 miles from Kandy. He spent fifteen days of every month traveling to evaluate each plantation. The rest of his time he spent working from home.

Gardening was one of his favorite activities to do in those periods between trips. In fact, both of my grandparents were prolific gardeners, growing okra, carrots, cabbage, leeks, pumpkin, eggplant, avocado, rhubarb, mango, papaya, banana, pomegranates, passion fruit, coconut, clove, cardamom, nutmeg, peppercorn, cocoa, ginger, and vanilla—and I'm sure that I'm forgetting something. It was always the stories of the vanilla that interested me, since apparently my grandfather and I shared a deep appreciation for fresh vanilla beans. He grew vanilla orchids all throughout the family garden, just for the pleasure of eating fresh, homegrown vanilla.

My father and his brothers and sisters were often put to work in the garden and with the plants. Once, after my dad and his little sister broke a branch off a poinsettia tree for fun, my grandfather made them stand in the yard holding the large branch between them, up over their heads, as punishment. The time ticked on slowly as their shoulders grew tired and the sun beat down on the tops of their heads. They never underestimated the importance of the plants and trees in the garden again.

The vanilla orchid is an especially finicky plant. Each pale yellow flower blooms only once, and only for a few hours. If it's not pollinated during that time, it quickly begins to wilt and die. Only pollinated orchids grow vanilla beans. So to cultivate a vanilla bean, a person, a bird, or an insect must pollinate the blooming flower.

My grandfather enlisted his children to do this job. Every day, during the two months when the orchids would flower, my dad, or one of his siblings, would walk through the garden to inspect the vanilla creepers that snaked up the plumeria trees. Different plants would be flowering on different days, and it was imperative to check every day. If he saw one flowering, the real work began.

With a piece of coconut straw pulled from the ekel brooms that my grandmother used to sweep the shiny concrete floors, my father would carefully lift the tiny shield covering the flower's stigma and press the anther, which contains the pollen, to the stigma. If he succeeded, the bloom would shrivel and turn brown and eventually the stem would elongate downward into a long, green pod. After six to nine months of ripening, my grandmother would pick and cure the beans, drying them in the sun during the day and covering them at night, until they were ready for use. She used them in tea blends, and especially in custards, until the following year, when the orchids bloomed again, and the cycle started anew.

A TRICKY FLOWER

Vanilla orchids are the only plants in the entire orchid family that produce edible fruit. That's one special flower! But the secret to unlocking the flower's potential remained hidden for hundreds of years.

The vanilla orchid is native to Central America and was first cultivated by the native Indians of Mexico. They used vanilla as early as 2,500 years before the Spanish conquest of Mexico in 1520. Mayan and Aztec recipes for chocolate include plenty of fragrant vanilla.

After the conquest, vanilla orchid cuttings were taken around the world. The plants thrived and flowered, but in only a few documented instances did the flowers actually go on to produce a seedpod. The plant frustrated all those who tried to profit from it. It wasn't until the mid-1800s when one little boy made an important discovery. All dessert lovers owe a debt of gratitude to Edmond Albius.

In 1841, on the French island of Réunion (formerly Bourbon) lived an amateur botanist named Ferréol Bellier-Beaumont. He loved to experiment with decorative plants and commercial fruits and vegetables. Edmond Albius was his slave and his houseboy.

Twelve-year-old Edmond was interested in plants too. He took to following his master around the estate to observe his experiments and ministrations. Bellier-Beaumont was more than happy to teach young Edmond his ways with plants, and the boy seemed to have an aptitude for botany.

Among his many plants, Bellier-Beaumont grew vanilla orchids. While he enjoyed the pale yellow flowers, he had the same problem with the delicate flowers as so many before him. The coveted vanilla seedpods were practically impossible to get. It was Edmond who finally came up with the solution.

During his rounds in the garden, Bellier-Beaumont taught Edmond about watermelon plants and the special pollination technique used to marry male and female flowers. Clever Edmond noticed that each vanilla orchid flower had similar male and female elements. He realized that the key was to marry the male and female parts in each vanilla flower. He used a bamboo splinter to pollinate the orchid.

Some days later, Edmond's vanilla orchid started to elongate and take shape. Bellier-Beaumont invited other landowners to come to his estate to learn of Edmond's technique—and the rest is the history of good things to eat. By 1848, only seven years later, the island of Réunion exported fifty kilos of vanilla pods to France. In 1867, they exported twenty tons—in 1898, two hundred tons! Edmond's discovery ignited vanilla production from Indonesia to Tahiti and back to Mexico.

Edmond was freed from slavery in 1848, but he never received any payment for his contribution to the vanilla trade and the dessert business. Instead, Edmond went on to find menial work as a laborer, and even spent some time in prison under dubious circumstances. Bellier-Beaumont tried to acquire a state pension for his favorite protégé, but his requests went unanswered. Yet he never stopped trying to get Edmond the recognition he deserved.

I can't help but think that the year my grandfather taught my dad how to hand-pollinate the family vanilla orchids and the year of Edmond's innovation weren't much more than a hundred years apart. Neither my family nor my desserts would be the same without Edmond's discovery.

WHAT ARE VANILLA BEANS?

Vanilla beans are the fruit of the flowering vanilla orchid, *Vanilla planifolia*, native to Mexico and Central America. The commercial process for growing and curing vanilla plants is a lot more complicated than that used by Edmond and my grandparents. Six months after fertilization the long, green pods turn yellow. At that point, they are exposed to high temperatures to prevent further maturation. The beans are wrapped in blankets to create humid conditions and sweat them. The resulting enzymatic reactions produce vanillin, the compound that gives vanilla its distinct flavor and aroma. Then the pods turn brown and supple. Finally, the beans are dried and stored for several months to further develop the flavor. Only then are they ready for sale.

BUYING AND STORING

Vanilla beans are worth the expense—and buying them in bulk from an online source, like www.beanilla.com or www.penzeys.com, makes them much more affordable. Store the plump, sticky beans in an airtight container in a dark place and they'll last for years. Don't store them in the fridge as the moisture can cause mold to grow.

Bourbon? Tahitian? Mexican? Which vanilla bean is best? Different beans grown in different parts of the world will have slightly different flavors, so it's best (and fun) to experiment and see which you prefer. Some say that Bourbon beans, from Madagascar and Réunion, have a hay-like sweetness, while Mexican beans are a bit spicy, and Tahitian more floral. As long as they're good-quality beans, they will be delicious, so feel free to experiment.

To use a vanilla bean, lay it flat on a cutting board and use a sharp paring knife to slice the bean lengthwise. Using the dull side of the knife, scrape the seeds from the two sides of the split pod. The pods themselves have a lot of flavor, so even if the recipe doesn't call for the pod, don't throw it away. Empty pods can be used to add flavor to granulated sugar, loose tea, or even a pitcher of lemonade or a pot of hot cider.

Pure vanilla extract is made by soaking vanilla beans in alcohol and aging the liquor. The higher the alcohol content, the more intense the vanilla flavor. A good rule of thumb is that one tablespoon of vanilla extract equals one fresh vanilla bean.

Vanilla bean paste is sweetened vanilla extract with ground beans. In a pinch, this works as a substitute for fresh beans in a custard or ice cream where visible seeds are a plus but the flavor is inferior. The beans have already been used once, and they are added to the mixture mostly for the visual effect.

I don't recommend the use of imitation vanilla extract. Its synthetic flavor will never compare to the real stuff and isn't worth using. The good news is that imitation vanilla is always clearly labeled and easy to avoid.

BLACKBERRY CUATRO LECHES

SERVES 12

Unsalted butter, for greasing the pan

12 ounces (about 2½ cups) fresh blackberries

1½ cups (6¾ ounces) all-purpose flour

1½ teaspoons baking powder

½ teaspoon kosher salt

4 large eggs, separated

¾ cup sugar

⅓ cup plus ¾ cup whole milk

1 vanilla bean, split and seeds scraped

¾ cup condensed milk

¾ cup evaporated milk

¾ cup heavy cream

1 teaspoon pure vanilla extract

Tres leches cake has a long history in my family. Ages ago, my mom bought a tres leches cake from the supermarket. She and my dad went nuts for it. But, because they never studied Romance languages, and the name was so unfamiliar to their ears, they forgot it completely. They would always describe this outstanding dessert with such vigor and enthusiasm—but because they had no idea what it was called, they could never find it again. My brother and I were understandably desperate to taste this magical cake, but they couldn't tell us what it was. Our search went on for years. You think I'm kidding. I wish I were. Only after studying Spanish in college and a chance encounter with the dessert at a restaurant was I able to put the puzzle together.

Fortunately, I can now bake myself a tres leches cake whenever I want. What a relief. The name refers to the three types of dairy (condensed milk, evaporated milk, and heavy cream) that make up the creamy sauce that soaks into the cake. I like milk so much that I've started using four. The addition of whole milk cuts some of the sweetness and renders the sauce exactly rich enough. Blackberries add a welcome tartness and striking color. A double dose of vanilla, in the form of both extract and fresh beans, adds a delightful floral essence that complements the fruit and sauce beautifully.

Preheat the oven to 350°F. Butter the bottom of an 8-inch square baking pan.

Cut 6 ounces of the blackberries in half lengthwise and set aside.

In a small bowl, whisk together the flour, baking powder, and salt. In a large bowl, with an electric mixer, beat the egg yolks and ½ cup of the sugar on medium speed until pale and thick, 3 to 4 minutes. Beat in ⅓ cup of the whole milk and the vanilla seeds. Beat in the flour mixture, just until combined.

CONTINUED

In a large bowl, with clean beaters, whip the egg whites until foamy and the yellowish hue has disappeared, about 1 minute. Slowly add the remaining ¼ cup sugar while beating and continue to beat the mixture until you have shiny, medium-stiff peaks, about 2 minutes. Stir one-quarter of the egg white mixture into the flour mixture to loosen it. Use a rubber spatula to gently fold the remaining whites into the batter.

Pour the batter into the prepared pan and scatter the halved blackberries on top. Bake until golden brown and a toothpick inserted into the cake comes out clean, 35 to 40 minutes. Let cool on a rack for 5 minutes.

Meanwhile in a medium bowl, combine the remaining ¾ cup whole milk, the condensed milk, the evaporated milk, the heavy cream, and the vanilla extract. Cut around the edges of the cake. With a toothpick, poke holes all over the cake. Pour about 1 cup of the milk mixture evenly over the cake and let it soak in. Then pour another 1 cup over the cake. Cover and chill the cake for at least 4 hours or up to overnight.

Serve slices of the cake with the remaining milk mixture and remaining blackberries. Store leftovers, well-wrapped, in the refrigerator for up to 2 days.

CREAM TEA BRÛLÉE

SERVES 4

1 cup heavy cream

½ cup whole milk

1 vanilla bean, split and seeds scraped

1 tablespoon loose Earl Grey tea

3 large egg yolks

6 tablespoons sugar

Pinch of kosher salt

Ceylon tea is one of the commodities that made the island famous, and is a justly ubiquitous staple in everyday life there. My dad's mother used to make her own special blend. She would always take at least one of the vanilla beans that they cultivated from orchids, split it, and set it in the canister that held the tea leaves. The essence of vanilla perfumed the tea leaves. Homegrown tea and homegrown vanilla—extraordinary.

This recipe was inspired by her. I use Earl Grey tea to flavor the cream, because the subtle citrus flavor of the bergamot makes a perfect complement to the vanilla.

A small culinary blowtorch is the best tool for evenly caramelizing the sugar on top of these custards. The broiler works, but be careful not to overcook the custard or burn the sugar.

Preheat the oven to 325°F. Put 4 shallow (¾-inch deep) 4-ounce crème brûlée ramekins in a baking pan. Set a fine-mesh sieve over a 2-cup liquid measuring cup.

In a medium saucepan, bring the cream, milk, and vanilla bean and seeds just to a boil over medium-high heat. Remove from the heat and stir in the tea. Let stand, covered, for 10 minutes. Bring a kettle of water to a boil.

Meanwhile, in a large bowl, whisk together the egg yolks, 3 tablespoons of the sugar, and salt until well combined.

Add about a third of the cream mixture to the egg mixture and whisk to combine. Continue with this process, a third at a time, until the two are well combined. Strain the mixture through the sieve into the measuring cup. Divide the mixture among the ramekins and fill the baking pan with enough boiling water to reach halfway up the sides of the ramekins.

Bake until the edges of the custards are just set and the very center has a slight jiggle, 15 to 20 minutes. (Keep an eye on them; depending on the hot spots in your oven, you might have to take some out before the others are done.) Use tongs to remove the ramekins from the hot water and let cool on a rack.

Empty the baking pan of water and let cool. Set the custards back in the pan, wrap well with plastic wrap, and refrigerate at least 4 hours or up to 2 days. Putting them back in the pan makes it easy to wrap them in plastic without marring the surface of the custards.

Just before serving, remove the plastic wrap and sprinkle each custard evenly with a scant tablespoon of the remaining sugar. Light a mini blowtorch and hold the flame 2 to 3 inches from the top of the custard, slowly gliding it back and forth over the surface until the sugar melts and turns a deep golden brown. Allow the sugar to cool and harden for a few minutes. Serve immediately.

THE NEW CHOCOLATE CHIP COOKIE

MAKES ABOUT 2 DOZEN COOKIES

1 cup (4½ ounces) all-purpose flour

½ teaspoon baking soda

¾ teaspoon kosher salt

⅓ cup melted coconut oil

⅓ cup packed light brown sugar

¼ cup granulated sugar

2 tablespoons pure vanilla extract

1 large egg

4½ ounces bittersweet chocolate (60 to 70 percent cacao), chopped (about 1 cup)

2½ ounces (½ cup) shelled raw pistachios, coarsely chopped

1 cup (3 ounces) shredded unsweetened coconut, toasted (see page 10)

Flaky sea salt, for sprinkling (optional)

In Sri Lanka, coconut is in everything, sweet and savory alike. What else would you expect on a tropical island where big, beautiful coconuts grow on half the trees? It is tasty, nutritious, and even has magical healing properties. When I was a young, intrepid backyard-jungle explorer, I had more than a few unfortunate encounters with fire ants. I remember vividly how my grandmother's gentle application of coconut oil to the bites always eased the pain. I've been using coconut oil in my baking more and more lately. I swap it for butter to add some extra richness and healthy fat. The heavenly aroma is enough to take your breath away—and it always makes me feel cared for.

That's the spirit behind these cookies. They are unique enough to be strikingly delicious and familiar enough to please the staunchest traditionalist. I hope they'll become your family's new go-to cookie.

Preheat the oven to 350°F. Line two baking sheets with parchment paper.

In a medium bowl, whisk together the flour, baking soda, and salt. In a large bowl, using a wooden spoon, combine the coconut oil, brown sugar, and granulated sugar together until creamy. Stir in the vanilla and egg. Add the flour mixture to the coconut oil mixture and stir to combine. Fold in the chocolate, pistachios, and coconut.

Scoop the dough in 2-tablespoon scoops and place on the prepared baking sheets, at least 2 inches apart. Sprinkle each cookie with a bit of sea salt. Bake until golden brown, 12 to 14 minutes, rotating the sheets halfway through. Let the cookies cool on the sheets on racks for about 5 minutes.

I think these are best eaten warm, the day they're made. You can store them in an airtight container at room temperature for up to 2 days or in the freezer for up to a month. Make sure to let them cool completely before storing.

APRICOT RASPBERRY COBBLER WITH HAZELNUT BISCUITS

SERVES 8

FILLING

¼ cup sugar

1 vanilla bean, split and seeds scraped

1½ pounds (about 8 small) fresh apricots, pitted and cut into eighths

12 ounces (2½ cups) raspberries

1 tablespoon cornstarch

Pinch of kosher salt

TOPPING

2¼ ounces (½ cup) hazelnuts, toasted and skinned and cooled completely (see page 11)

1½ cups (6¾ ounces) all-purpose flour

½ cup granulated sugar

1 tablespoon baking powder

½ teaspoon kosher salt

½ cup (1 stick) cold unsalted butter, cut into pieces

½ cup cold heavy cream, plus more for brushing

¼ cup cold whole milk

Sanding sugar, for sprinkling

Perfectly ripe, in-season apricots have a distinct honey-like sweetness. Tossed with tart red raspberries and vanilla beans, they bubble into one of the most fragrant desserts you'll ever encounter. Toasty ground hazelnuts add another dimension to the biscuits, which develop beautiful crunchy tops, and soft, cakey interiors. If you don't have a food processor you can make the biscuits with 2¼ ounces of store-bought hazelnut meal.

Preheat the oven to 400°F. Have ready a 2-quart baking dish.

To prepare the filling, use your fingers to grind together the sugar and vanilla seeds until combined in a large bowl. Add the apricots, raspberries, cornstarch, and salt and fold to combine. Pour the mixture into the baking dish.

To prepare the biscuit topping, add the hazelnuts to the bowl of a food processor fitted with the metal blade and pulse until very finely ground, but stop before you've made a paste. Add the flour, sugar, baking powder, and salt, and pulse to combine. Add the butter and pulse until the mixture resembles coarse meal with a few pea-size pieces. Scrape the flour mixture into a medium bowl. (Pop the flour mixture into the refrigerator for a little while if the butter has gotten warm.) In a small bowl, combine the cream and milk and then, with a fork, stir it into the flour mixture just until evenly moistened. Don't overwork the dough.

Drop the dough in 8 to 10 apricot-size balls on top of the fruit mixture. Brush the tops of the dough balls with cream and sprinkle with sanding sugar. Bake until the fruit is bubbling, the topping is golden brown, and a toothpick inserted into the center of one biscuit comes out with moist crumbs attached, 40 to 45 minutes. Serve warm or at room temperature. Store leftovers well-wrapped in the fridge for up to 2 days. The biscuits will start to soften after the first day.

CRÊPE CAKE WITH PISTACHIO CREAM

SERVES 8

CRÊPES

4 large eggs plus 2 large egg yolks

2 cups whole milk

1/2 cup heavy cream

1 1/4 cups (5 5/8 ounces) all-purpose flour

3 tablespoons granulated sugar

1/2 teaspoon kosher salt

1/2 vanilla bean, split and seeds scraped

2 tablespoons (1/4 stick) unsalted butter, melted and cooled, plus more for greasing the skillet

CREAM

1 1/2 teaspoons unflavored powdered gelatin

3 tablespoons cold water

6 large egg yolks

3 1/2 ounces (about 6 tablespoons) pistachio paste

1/4 cup granulated sugar

1 tablespoon cornstarch

1/2 teaspoon kosher salt

1 1/2 cups whole milk

1/2 vanilla bean, split and seeds scraped

1 tablespoon unsalted butter

1 cup heavy cream

2 tablespoons confectioners' sugar

TO FINISH

2 tablespoons granulated sugar

Impressive but simple. That's really the key to the perfect party dessert, and crêpe cake fits the bill. All the parts can be made in advance—in fact, it's better if you do so—and on the evening of the celebration, all you have to do is eat and bask in the glory of your masterpiece.

Pistachio paste is a mixture of sugar and pistachios, often found in the baking aisle of a well-stocked supermarket or an Italian specialty market. Leftovers are delicious spread on toast or swirled into soft chocolate ice cream.

To prepare the crêpe batter, whisk together the eggs, egg yolks, milk, and cream in a medium bowl. In a large bowl, whisk together the flour, sugar, and salt. Make a large well in the center of the flour mixture and pour in the milk mixture. Gently whisk the center of the milk mixture, very gradually grabbing the flour around the edges, little by little, until it is all combined. Go slowly to avoid lumps. Alternatively, blend those ingredients in a blender until smooth. Strain the mixture into a clean bowl and whisk in the vanilla bean and seeds and the butter. Cover and refrigerate overnight.

To prepare the cream, sprinkle the gelatin over the water and let it stand for 10 minutes. In a medium saucepan, whisk together the egg yolks, pistachio paste, sugar, cornstarch, and salt. Slowly whisk in the milk. Stir in the vanilla bean and seeds. Cook over medium-low heat, stirring constantly and making sure to get the edges, until the mixture begins to thicken, 4 to 6 minutes. (Switch between a whisk and a spatula for the best results.) Let it come up to a slow boil and cook for 2 minutes more. Add the gelatin mixture and stir until the gelatin is completely melted, about 1 minute. Strain the cream mixture through a fine-mesh sieve into a clean bowl and add the butter. Cover with plastic wrap, making sure the plastic touches the surface of the cream, and refrigerate until completely cold, about 2 hours. Whip the heavy cream

CONTINUED

and confectioners' sugar to medium-stiff peaks. Fold the whipped cream into the chilled pastry cream. Cover with plastic wrap touching the surface of the cream and chill well, at least 4 hours (or up to overnight).

Stir the crêpe batter well and discard the vanilla bean. Melt a little bit of butter in a 10-inch nonstick skillet over medium heat and let the pan get hot. Remove the pan from the heat and immediately add a scant ¼ cup (about 3 tablespoons) crêpe batter to one side of the pan. Quickly tilt and swirl the pan to spread the batter to an even thickness. Return the pan to the heat and cook until very lightly golden and set on one side, about 30 seconds. Tuck a small offset spatula under the edge of the crêpe, grab onto it with your fingers, and quickly flip it over. Cook until light golden brown on the other side, 30 seconds to 1 minute. Slip the crêpe onto a parchment-lined baking sheet to cool.

Continue with the rest of the batter, stirring between crêpes and occasionally wiping out the skillet with a paper towel. Very lightly butter the skillet every few crêpes. The batter should make about 20 crêpes but you only need 15 for the cake, so don't worry if a couple go wrong or you have to taste a few. You can stack the crêpes once they're cool, but spread them out until then.

Stir the pistachio cream to make it smooth and spreadable. Lay one cooled crêpe on a cake platter or plate. Spread ¼ cup pistachio cream on top and then top with another crêpe. Spread the cream slightly thicker around the edges so that the finished cake is level. Repeat this process until you've stacked 15 crêpes with cream. Make sure to finish with a pretty crêpe on top. Cover lightly with plastic wrap and chill it for at least 4 hours or up to 1 day.

To serve, sprinkle the top of the cake with the 2 tablespoons of sugar. Light a mini blowtorch and hold the flame 2 to 3 inches from the top of the cake, slowly gliding it back and forth over the surface until the sugar melts and turns a deep golden brown. Allow the sugar to cool and harden for a few minutes. Serve immediately. (You can skip this last step if you don't have a mini blowtorch.) Store leftovers in the fridge, well wrapped, for up to 2 days.

STRAWBERRY THYME SEMIFREDDO

SERVES 8

2 pounds strawberries, hulled and sliced (4 cups)

½ cup plus 1 tablespoon sugar

4 sprigs thyme, plus 1 teaspoon chopped fresh thyme

1 vanilla bean, split and seeds scraped

Pinch of kosher salt

4 large egg yolks

1¼ cups heavy cream

Semifreddo, which means "half-cold" in Italian, is a semifrozen cross between ice cream and mousse. The beauty of a semifreddo, besides the pleasure you get from eating it, is the fact that you can make it completely by hand, with just a whisk and a bit of elbow grease. I like the sweet, fragrant, and herbal combination of vanilla, strawberries, and thyme, but basil or mint would be excellent too.

In a medium saucepan, combine 3 cups of the strawberries, ¼ cup of the sugar, 4 sprigs thyme, the vanilla bean and seeds, and salt. Cook the mixture over medium heat just until the strawberries begin to soften slightly, about 4 minutes. Remove from the heat and let cool to room temperature. Remove the thyme sprigs and vanilla bean and process the strawberry mixture in a food processor until somewhat smooth. Stir in the chopped thyme.

In a large bowl over a pot of very barely simmering water, whisk together the egg yolks and ¼ cup of the sugar. Make sure the bottom of the bowl isn't touching the water. Using an electric mixer or with a large whisk, still with the bowl held over the simmering water, beat the yolk mixture until pale yellow, thick, and doubled in volume, 3 to 5 minutes. Remove from the heat and beat the yolk mixture another minute, then fold in the strawberry mixture.

Beat the cream to medium-stiff peaks. Fold the cream into the strawberry mixture. Pour the strawberry mixture into a loaf pan lined with plastic wrap. Fold the plastic wrap over the top to cover completely. Freeze until firm, at least 6 hours.

When ready to serve, toss the remaining 1 cup of sliced strawberries with the remaining tablespoon of sugar. Let the semifreddo stand at room temperature for 5 to 10 minutes. Unwrap and invert the semifreddo onto a serving plate, remove the plastic, and top with the strawberries. Cut the semifreddo into slices and serve. Store leftovers well wrapped in the freezer.

CUSTARD CAKE WITH CHOCOLATE AND PRUNES

SERVES 10

CUSTARD
3 large egg yolks

1/3 cup granulated sugar

3 tablespoons cornstarch

3/4 cup whole milk

3/4 cup heavy cream

1 vanilla bean, split and seeds scraped

1 tablespoon butter

CAKE
1/2 cup (1 stick) unsalted butter, at room temperature, plus more for greasing the pan

13/4 cups (77/8 ounces) all-purpose flour

11/2 teaspoons baking powder

3/4 teaspoon kosher salt

2/3 cup packed light brown sugar

2 large eggs

1/4 cup whole milk

11/2 teaspoons pure vanilla extract

4 ounces bittersweet chocolate (60 to 70 percent cacao), chopped (about 1 cup)

4 ounces (3/4 cup) chopped pitted prunes

Confectioners' sugar, for serving

My parents' living room is full of reading material. Everywhere you look, there are magazine holders, crammed full. Upon closer inspection, you'll notice that surprisingly, the racks don't hold many current titles. They're filled with old issues of *Everyday Food* and *Fine Cooking* from my time as a food editor, along with some yellowed *Good Housekeeping* magazines from the early 1980s. I love flipping through those old ones. I can remember looking at the very same copies when I was small, drooling over the peach melbas and the mud pies. And the puddings.

One vivid advertisement suggested that moms (always moms) make a sheet cake, poke holes in it with the handle of a wooden spoon, and fill it with either flavored gelatin or pudding. A close-up of a cross-section of a slice revealed long stalactites of glorious gels piercing the fluffy cake. Classic.

Those cakes were the inspiration for this one. The creamy vanilla custard is swirled throughout the cake batter, leaving luscious pockets to discover while eating.

Set a fine-mesh sieve over a large bowl.

To prepare the custard, stir together the egg yolks, sugar, and cornstarch in a medium bowl until smooth. In a medium saucepan, bring the milk, heavy cream, and vanilla bean and seeds to a simmer over medium heat. Add a little bit of the warm milk mixture to the yolk mixture and whisk to combine. Repeat this process a few times until all of the milk mixture has been incorporated into the yolk mixture.

Return the mixture to the pan. Cook over medium-low heat, stirring constantly and making sure to get the edges, until the mixture begins to thicken, 2 to 4 minutes. (It's helpful to have both a spatula and a whisk handy while making the custard. Switch between the two.) Let it come up to a very slow boil and cook for 1 minute more. Strain the custard through the sieve into the bowl, and stir in the butter. Press plastic wrap onto the surface of the cream and refrigerate until cooled completely.

Preheat the oven to 325°F. Butter a 9-inch springform pan.

To prepare the cake, stir the chilled custard to loosen it a bit. In a small bowl, whisk together the flour, baking powder, and salt. In a large bowl, with an electric mixer, beat the butter and brown sugar on medium speed until fluffy, 3 to 4 minutes. Beat in the eggs, one at a time, scraping down the bowl in between. Beat in the flour mixture then the milk and the vanilla extract. Fold in the chocolate and the prunes. The batter will be thick.

Using an offset spatula, spread half of the cake batter evenly in the prepared pan. Top with the custard in dollops. Using the spatula, swirl the cake batter and the custard a few times to intersperse it. No need to make decorative swirls. The goal is to combine the two just enough to get thick ribbons of custard running through the batter. You do not want an evenly combined mixture. Top with dollops of the remaining cake batter and spread it out, covering the custard layer as best as you can. Don't worry. You can't make any mistakes. It will look messy and taste delicious.

Bake until a toothpick inserted into the center comes out with moist crumbs attached, 35 to 45 minutes. Cool slightly on a rack and then remove the pan edge. Dust with confectioners' sugar to serve.

This cake is best eaten warm, but leftovers can be stored in an airtight container at room temperature for up to 2 days.

MARMALADE CAKES

MAKES 12 CAKES

MARMALADE

2 small seedless
navel oranges (5 to
6 ounces each)

¾ cup sugar

1 vanilla bean, split and
seeds scraped

1¼ cups water

CAKES

1 cup (4½ ounces)
all-purpose flour

¾ cup (4 ounces)
fine-ground yellow
cornmeal

1½ teaspoons baking
powder

½ teaspoon kosher salt

¾ cup (1½ sticks) unsalted
butter, at room temperature

¾ cup sugar

2 teaspoons finely grated
lemon zest (from 1 lemon)

2 large eggs, at room
temperature

⅔ cup buttermilk,
at room temperature

These buttery, tangy corn cakes are pretty enough for a party but not so sweet that you couldn't enjoy one for breakfast. While a traditional marmalade rarely includes vanilla beans, I find that their creamy aroma is right at home with the oranges and sugar. In earlier versions of this recipe, I made the quick marmalade and added it all to the cake batter. The results were delicious, but they needed a visual boost. I remembered a gorgeous photograph I had seen when I worked as a food editor for Martha Stewart. In one of her cookbooks, there is an image of a cupcake with a candied orange slice perched on top. There was my solution. I reserved twelve orange slices from the marmalade mixture and put them on top of the cakes after baking. Now they're gorgeous and tasty.

Cut an 11-inch circle of parchment paper. Cut a small hole in the center of the circle.

To prepare the marmalade, slice off the ends of each orange and discard. Slice each orange into 9 rounds, about ⅛ inch thick. Stir together the sugar, vanilla bean and seeds, and water in a 10-inch skillet. Bring the mixture to a simmer over medium-high heat, stirring to dissolve the sugar. Add the orange slices and place the parchment circle directly on top of the fruit and the liquid. (This keeps the moisture locked in and the fruit submerged in the syrup.) Decrease the heat to low to maintain a very gentle simmer. Cook until the slices are almost translucent and the liquid is the consistency of maple syrup, 35 to 45 minutes. Flip the slices over every so often to make sure they are all being cooked evenly. Add a little more water if the level gets too low before the slices are cooked. Let the mixture stand off the heat until cool enough to handle.

Reserve 12 slices of the same circumference and the syrup for later. Finely chop the remaining slices.

CONTINUED

Preheat the oven to 350°F. Line a standard 12-cup muffin tin with paper liners.

To prepare the cakes, whisk together the flour, cornmeal, baking powder, and salt in a small bowl. In a large bowl, with an electric mixer, beat the butter and sugar on medium speed until fluffy, 3 to 4 minutes. Add the chopped orange and the lemon zest and beat to combine. Beat in the eggs, one at a time. Beat in half of the flour mixture, then the buttermilk, then the remaining flour mixture.

Divide the batter among the cupcake cups and bake until a toothpick inserted into the center comes out with moist crumbs attached, 16 to 18 minutes. Let cakes cool in the tin for 10 minutes, then transfer them to a rack to cool completely. Top each cake with a reserved orange slice and brush the orange slices with the reserved syrup.

These are best served the day they're made, but you can store leftovers in an airtight container at room temperature for up to 2 days.

ROASTED BANANA ICE CREAM WITH BITTERSWEET CHOCOLATE

MAKES ABOUT 1 QUART

3 cups heavy cream

2 vanilla beans, split and seeds scraped

1 tablespoon unsalted butter

½ cup packed dark brown sugar

3 tablespoons water

4 extra-ripe bananas (about 1¼ pounds), peeled (thawed if frozen)

6 large egg yolks

½ teaspoon kosher salt

1 teaspoon pure vanilla extract

5 ounces bittersweet chocolate (60 to 70 percent cacao), chopped (about 1¼ cups)

This is the perfect recipe for using those forgotten bananas that have been languishing on the countertop for too long. Sometimes we'd all like something other than banana bread! I like to peel and freeze overripe fruit for a rainy day. This recipe works exceptionally well with bananas that have been frozen and thawed. All their wonderful juices mingle with the brown sugar and butter as soon as they meet in the pan. The finished product is like a sophisticated banana split wrapped up in a single scoop.

Preheat the oven to 450°F.

In a medium saucepot, stir together 2 cups of the heavy cream and the vanilla beans and seeds. Bring to a simmer over medium heat then remove from the heat, cover, and set aside to infuse, 30 minutes to 1 hour.

In a 12-inch ovenproof skillet, melt the butter over medium heat. Add the sugar and the water. Stir to combine. (Thawed frozen bananas let out a lot of juice. Use that liquid in place of water for extra tastiness.) Add the bananas, gently toss them to coat, and then put the skillet in the oven. Bake until the sugar is bubbling and the bananas have softened and collapsed, 25 to 30 minutes, stirring halfway through. Put the banana mixture in the bowl of a food processor fitted with the metal blade and process until smooth (make sure to scrape in all of that wonderful sauce from the skillet!). Pour the banana mixture into a medium bowl to cool. (You should have about 1¼ cups puree. Any extra puree makes a delicious spread for toast.) Set a fine-mesh sieve over the bowl of banana puree.

In a medium bowl, whisk together the egg yolks and salt. Add the cream mixture to the yolk mixture and whisk to combine. Return the cream mixture to the pot and cook over medium-low heat, stirring constantly, until the mixture is just thick enough to coat the back of a spoon,

CONTINUED

6 to 8 minutes. It's important not to let the mixture come to a boil or it will curdle. For this reason, it's better to take it off the heat too early rather than too late.

Fill a bowl larger than the bowl of puree partway with ice water.

Strain the custard through the sieve set over the bowl of banana puree, discarding any solids. Whisk in the vanilla extract and remaining cup of cream. Set the bowl into the bowl of ice water. Stir occasionally until completely chilled and very thick. You can sneak a few spoonfuls at this point; the eggs are completely cooked.

Freeze in an ice cream maker according to the manufacturer's instructions, adding the chocolate during the last minute of processing. Spoon into a freezer-proof container and freeze until firm, at least 8 hours. Let the ice cream sit at room temperature for about 10 minutes before serving. Store in an airtight container (with an extra layer of plastic pressed directly onto the surface of the ice cream) in the freezer for up to 2 weeks.

SESAME JAM BUTTER BUTTONS

MAKES ABOUT 2½ DOZEN COOKIES

½ cup (2½ ounces) white sesame seeds

1 vanilla beans, split and seeds scraped

6 tablespoons sugar

1 cup (4½ ounces) all-purpose flour

½ teaspoon baking powder

½ teaspoon kosher salt

½ cup (1 stick) unsalted butter, at room temperature

1 large egg

1 teaspoon pure vanilla extract

⅓ cup raspberry jam

"Open Sesame!" Everyone knows the phrase that Ali Baba spoke to open the cave filled with treasures in *The Arabian Nights*. Some say that it refers to the fact that when sesame seeds are fully ripe, the pods burst open, just as Ali Baba hoped the cave would. These cookie gems are a treasure in themselves. The sesame and fruit are lovely together, with the slight bitterness of the seeds offsetting the sweetness of the jam and the vanilla.

Line two baking sheets with parchment paper. Preheat the oven to 350°F. Add the sesame seeds to a small skillet and heat over medium heat, stirring often, until fragrant, about 10 minutes. Pour the seeds onto a plate to cool completely.

Using a spice grinder, process ¼ cup of the sesame seeds, the vanilla bean seeds, and 1 tablespoon of the sugar until finely ground. In a medium bowl, whisk together the ground sesame seed mixture, flour, baking powder, and salt. In a large bowl, stir the butter and the remaining 5 tablespoons of sugar until creamy. Stir in the egg and the vanilla extract. Add the flour mixture to the butter mixture and stir to combine. Set aside 2 teaspoons of the sesame seeds for sprinkling and stir in the remaining sesame seeds. Pop the dough into the fridge for a few minutes to chill and firm up.

Drop the dough in 1-tablespoon scoops 1 inch apart on the prepared sheets. Bake until the cookies are light golden and just set, 6 to 8 minutes. Remove the sheets from the oven and carefully make a well in each cookie using the bowl of a 1-teaspoon measuring spoon. Fill each cookie well with ½ teaspoon of jam. Return the sheets to the oven, making sure to rotate them, and bake until the cookies are golden brown around the edges, 6 to 8 minutes. Let the cookies cool, still on the baking sheets, on racks. While the cookies are still warm, sprinkle them with the remaining 2 teaspoons sesame seeds. Store in an airtight container at room temperature for up to 3 days or in the freezer for up to a month.

PAVLOVA WITH LIME CUSTARD AND BASIL PINEAPPLE

SERVES 8

MERINGUE
½ vanilla bean, split and seeds scraped

¾ cup sugar

4 large egg whites, at room temperature

1 teaspoon distilled white vinegar

1½ teaspoons cornstarch

CUSTARD
2 large egg yolks

3 tablespoons sugar

1½ teaspoons cornstarch

Pinch of kosher salt

1 cup heavy cream

½ vanilla bean, split and seeds scraped

¼ cup fresh lime juice (from 2 limes)

TO FINISH
½ medium pineapple, peeled, cored, and thinly sliced into bite-size pieces (about 2 cups)

1 tablespoon chopped fresh basil leaves

¼ teaspoon grated lime zest (from 1 lime)

Traditional pavlova is made by topping a large baked meringue with whipped cream and fruit. It was created in the early twentieth century to honor the Russian ballet dancer Anna Pavlova. Perhaps the baker was inspired, after watching Pavlova perform, to create something lighter than air. A perfect meringue is exactly that. It's a cloud-like puff, complete with an appealing crunchy exterior and a chewy center. I top mine with a tart lime custard to balance out the sweetness of the meringue, and plenty of fresh pineapple and basil. The combination is unexpected and wonderful.

Meringue is simple to prepare but takes a few hours to bake. If you make it the day before you plan to serve it, you can leave it to dry out in the oven overnight. Meringue is best undertaken when the air is dry, and avoided at other times. Humidity makes meringue (and bakers) weep.

Preheat the oven to 350°F. Line a baking sheet with parchment paper. Using a cake pan or a plate, trace an 8-inch circle on the paper. Flip the paper over and set on the sheet.

To prepare the meringue, in a small bowl, use your fingers to blend the vanilla seeds into the sugar until evenly combined. In a large bowl, with an electric mixer, whip the egg whites on medium-high until foamy and the yellowish hue has disappeared, about 1 minute. With the mixer running, add the vanilla sugar and continue to beat until you have shiny, stiff peaks, about 4 minutes. Quickly beat in the vinegar and then the cornstarch. Spoon the mixture onto the prepared parchment sheet and swirl the meringue decoratively within the 8-inch circle. Place in the oven and immediately decrease the oven temperature to 250°F.

Bake the meringue until the outside is very crisp, about 90 minutes. Check the meringue every 25 minutes. If it is taking on too much color, decrease the oven temperature

CONTINUED

by 25 degrees. When finished, it will be slightly off-white. Turn the oven off and let the meringue stand inside until completely cooled. Overnight is just fine—as long as it isn't a humid day.

Set a fine-mesh sieve over a large bowl.

To prepare the custard, whisk together the egg yolks, sugar, cornstarch, and salt in a medium bowl. In a small saucepan, heat ½ cup of the heavy cream and the vanilla bean seeds over medium-low heat until hot. While whisking, add the hot cream into the egg yolk mixture. Return the mixture back into the saucepan and stir in the lime juice. Continue to cook, stirring constantly, until just bubbling. Let it cook 1 minute more. Strain the custard through the sieve into the bowl. Cover with plastic wrap, pressing it onto the surface, and chill until cold.

Just before serving, toss the pineapple with the basil and lime zest. Whip the remaining ½ cup cream to soft peaks. Fold the whipped cream into the custard. Spread the custard cream evenly over the top of the meringue, leaving a 1-inch border. Top with the pineapple mixture and serve immediately. Pavlova is best eaten as soon as it is assembled.

COCONUT MANGO TAPIOCA PUDDING

SERVES 4 TO 6

1 cup water

2 ounces (⅓ cup) small pearl tapioca

1¾ cups coconut milk

¾ cup whole milk plus 1 to 2 tablespoons, if necessary

¼ cup sugar

1 vanilla bean, split and seeds scraped

Pinch of kosher salt

2 large egg yolks

½ teaspoon pure vanilla extract

2 cups diced fresh mango (from 2 small mangoes)

Tapioca pudding is one of those truly divisive dishes: you either love it or you hate it. I think it's just wonderful. An affinity for cassava is actually in my genes. My grandmother grew it in the family garden and my dad loved it so much that he used to munch on the starchy root raw!

Made from starch of the cassava root, chewy tapioca pearls add a pleasant pop to this pudding. It's perfect with naturally sweet coconut milk. Make sure your mango is very ripe, so the juices run off and create an aromatic, juicy swirl.

In a small bowl, add the water to the tapioca. Let stand at room temperature for 30 minutes. Drain and add the tapioca to a medium saucepan.

Add the coconut milk, whole milk, sugar, vanilla bean seeds, and salt. Bring to a boil over medium-high heat, stirring occasionally, and then decrease the heat to low to maintain a very low simmer. Make sure to scrape the bottom of the pan, as the tapioca tends to stick. Cook the mixture until the tapioca is swollen and the milk mixture is thick, stirring often, 7 to 8 minutes.

Remove from the heat. Add the egg yolks to a small bowl. Add about ½ cup of the hot pudding to the egg yolks while whisking. Repeat this process a couple of times to warm up the egg yolks. Add the egg yolk mixture to the saucepan and stir to combine. Heat over low heat, stirring, until thickened, 1 to 2 minutes. Remove from the heat and stir in the vanilla extract. Pour into a large bowl and let cool to room temperature.

Fold in the mango. Cover with plastic wrap pressed onto the surface of the pudding and chill at least 6 hours. You can stir 1 or 2 tablespoons of milk into the cold pudding if you'd like a looser consistency. Store the pudding in the refrigerator, in an airtight container, for up to 3 days.

CHAPTER 6

ginger

I give ginger credit for changing the course of my life. More specifically, gingerbread. When I first made Regan Daley's Black Sticky Gingerbread from her fantastic baking compendium *In the Sweet Kitchen*, I saw ginger, and myself, in a new light.

At the time, I was a recent college graduate, and like so many other recent grads, I had only a vague plan for my life. I loved to bake, but I never thought that I could make a career of it. That's where Regan and her gingerbread came in.

I spent weekends reading and bookmarking her book, shopping and baking. That recipe spoke to me, and inspired me to bake and rebake it time and again. First and foremost, that cake is all about ginger. Some gingerbread merely hints at the spice, letting the sweeteners take the lead. But hers has both fresh ginger, adding a bright spiciness (which I always increased, never willing to leave well enough alone), as well as ground ginger for mellow heat. In addition to that, it has the perfect crust and tender interior, a texture that only improves with age. I baked up countless batches of that cake, often putting my own spin on it, and sent it to my parents, walked it over to my brother's apartment, and brought it into work to share with my colleagues.

Even now, amid the magnets and pictures that clutter my parents' fridge, is an old yellow sticky note that reads, "Sticky Gingerbread for Sweet Mom and Sweet Dad. Keep it in the fridge so it becomes moist and delicious." There have been countless cakes since then, but those gingerbread days were significant. That note was a sign and they knew it.

Making a mess in my tiny New York apartment, sticky molasses on every surface and dirty dishes piled in the sink, I felt supremely content. Baking all those loaves of gingerbread, I realized that I had found my calling. I had declared my intention to be a baker when I was five years old, but it had taken twenty more years to take my five-year-old self seriously.

Watching my friends and family enjoy the gingerbread only deepened my resolve. I realized that feeding people cake was what I did best. I saw that a deep, dark spice cake made people deeply happy. I came to understand that I should really just be baking gingerbread for a living.

Or something like that. I kept working my day job in public television, went to culinary school at night, landed a job as a food editor at a magazine, and the rest is my dream life come true.

GINGER THROUGH THE AGES

Ginger is thought to be the oldest spice. So old, in fact, that early cultivation predates historical records. This makes it tricky to pinpoint ginger's origin and track its spread around the globe. Some historians believe that the very fact that ginger cannot spread by seed is a clue to its age. In order to grow new ginger, the horizontal root from which the plant grows (called the rhizome) must be split. Ginger cultivation has been under human control for so long that it has lost an essential characteristic of a wild plant, the ability to self-propagate. The flip side is that ginger is comparatively easy to spread and has grown well in other tropical and subtropical locations outside of its original home, so that compared to other spices, its progress across the globe was much simpler. Today it is the world's most widely cultivated spice.

Ginger probably originated in the tropics of Southeast Asia, and possibly India, where it was highly valued for its medicinal properties. Confucius was writing about ginger in the fifth century BC, and by that time it was also well known all over ancient Egypt, Greece, and Rome. By the end of the first century AD, ginger had spread throughout Europe, too. Most likely, the ginger that these ancient consumers knew was either dried or candied.

Ginger has also been linked to bread and baking for thousands of years. Historians believe that the earliest recipe for gingerbread dates to Greece in 2400 BC. Some say those early gingerbreads were used for ceremonial purposes, but I can't imagine the Greeks didn't sneak a nibble now and again.

By the Middle Ages, ginger was cultivated in parts of Southeast Asia, India, and Africa, and gingerbread had taken on an almost magical status. Gingerbread fairs were popping up all over Europe, ladies gave it to their knights before battle to protect them, and young women were downing it in hopes of luring a husband. It's no wonder that ginger was one of the spices Christopher Columbus was seeking. Single ladies all over Europe were eager for a taste and willing to pay.

Half a century after Columbus's spice mission to the New World, the Spanish crown granted the new American colonies, or New Spain, exclusive permission to plant black pepper, cloves, cinnamon, and ginger. Only ginger took. But it took with gusto. Within twenty years, the colonies were exporting over a thousand tons of fresh ginger to Europe. Today ginger is grown all over Asia, in parts of the United States, and in the Caribbean, but Jamaican ginger is said to be the world's best.

Some of that ginger likely made it over to Queen Elizabeth I, who ruled England in the sixteenth century. The woman loved dessert. Feasts in her honor were said to be lavishly filled with elaborate marzipan sculptures, jellies and marmalades, and an endless array of sweetmeats. But even among all these desserts, gingerbread stood out. The queen went so far as to keep a special baker among her staff who baked and molded gingerbread in the images of the guests of her court. Some say the gingerbread statues of dignitaries were life size. Others say that they were elaborately decorated gingerbread cookies. Either way, these early gingerbread men were certainly the precursor to the beloved, well-known Christmas cookies of today.

I love to imagine the queen handing out gingerbread portraits to her guests—I take comfort in the fact that I'm not the only person whose life has been shaped by ginger and its most famous application.

WHAT IS GINGER?

Ginger is a perennial tropical plant. The stalk, leaves, and the flowers are edible and can be used to flavor teas, soups, and rice, much like you would use lemongrass or bay leaves, but the ginger we are most familiar with is the rhizome of the plant. The genus *Zingiber* includes about eighty species and is probably indigenous to tropical India and Southeast Asia. Ginger is harvested twice annually. The first crop is the tender young rhizome. Young ginger is juicy with a pink hue and soft skin that doesn't need to be removed. Young ginger can be used interchangeably with mature ginger, but its mild-flavored flesh is best suited for more delicate applications. For example, young ginger makes outstanding candied ginger. The second harvest yields the more commonly available fibrous rhizomes with a stronger, spicier flavor.

BUYING AND STORING

Look for ginger with smooth firm skin and a fresh, spicy scent. Wrinkles and soft spots indicate a lack of freshness. Store unpeeled fresh ginger in the fridge for up to two weeks. To use fresh, mature ginger, peel off the skin using a vegetable peeler or a spoon and grate or chop the flesh. Fresh ginger has a citrusy bite and a sweet hotness. Mild young ginger doesn't need to be peeled before use. Since young ginger is harder to find, most recipes, including those in this book, are written for mature ginger. Be sure to increase the amount a bit if using young ginger. Ground ginger has less of that lemony flavor but plenty of wonderful aromatic heat. Ground ginger should last about 6 months in an airtight container. Both fresh and ground ginger have a place in the baker's kitchen, but neither is truly a substitute for the other.

BIG CHEWY APRICOT AND GINGER COOKIES

MAKES ABOUT 2 DOZEN COOKIES

2 cups (9 ounces) all-purpose flour

1 tablespoon ground ginger

2 teaspoons ground cinnamon

1 teaspoon baking soda

1/2 teaspoon freshly ground black pepper

1/2 teaspoon kosher salt

10 tablespoons (1¼ sticks) unsalted butter, at room temperature

1 cup granulated sugar

1 large egg

1/2 cup (3¼ ounces) crystallized ginger, finely chopped

1/3 cup unsulphured blackstrap molasses

2 tablespoons (1 ounce) peeled, finely grated fresh ginger

1 cup (6 ounces) dried whole apricots, chopped

Sanding sugar, for rolling (optional)

If you like things spicy, you'll love these cookies. With black pepper, ground ginger, fresh ginger, and crystallized ginger, these cookies pack a delicious punch—plenty of true ginger flavor. I like dried apricots in my ginger cookies for their aromatic, honey-like sweetness, but feel free to use raisins if you prefer.

Line two baking sheets with parchment paper.

In a large bowl, whisk together the flour, ground ginger, cinnamon, baking soda, pepper, and salt. In a second large bowl, using an electric mixer, beat the butter and sugar on medium speed until pale and fluffy, 3 to 4 minutes. Beat in the egg, crystallized ginger, molasses, and fresh ginger. With the mixer on low speed, beat in the flour mixture until combined. Stir in the apricots. Roll the dough in 3-tablespoon balls. (If the dough is too soft, pop it in the fridge to set up a bit.) Place the dough balls on one of the prepared sheets and chill until firm, covered, for at least 1 hour and up to overnight.

Preheat the oven to 350°F.

Roll each chilled ball in sanding sugar to coat, and then place on the prepared sheets, at least 2 inches apart (they will spread). Bake, rotating the sheets halfway through, until the center of each cookie is just set, 14 to 16 minutes. Let cool on baking sheets for 5 minutes, and then move the cookies to racks to cool completely.

Store the cookies in an airtight container at room temperature for up to 3 days or in the freezer for up to a month.

BUTTER RUM SNACK CAKE

MAKES 16 PIECES

½ cup (1 stick) unsalted butter, plus more for greasing the pan

6 tablespoons granulated sugar

⅓ cup packed dark brown sugar

3 tablespoons (1⅛ ounces) finely chopped crystallized ginger

2 tablespoons (½ ounce) peeled, minced, fresh ginger

1 large egg

¼ cup dark rum

2 teaspoons finely grated lime zest (from 1 lime)

1 teaspoon pure vanilla extract

1 cup (4½ ounces) all-purpose flour

½ teaspoon kosher salt

¼ teaspoon baking soda

3½ ounces roasted, salted macadamia nuts, chopped (about ¾ cup)

Two things happened on my first and only trip to Hawaii. First, the night we arrived I lost all the money that I had saved over a year of babysitting in one fell swoop. (I had decided that carrying all my cash in a wad in my pocket was a smart way to go. Not so, as it turned out.) Second, I discovered macadamia nuts and consoled myself with them for the rest of our family vacation. I developed a macadamia nut addiction on that trip. And I haven't grown out of it yet.

Macadamia nuts taste like nut-flavored butter, creamy and sweet and completely irresistible. This addictive snack cake pairs macadamias with plenty of ginger, lime, rum, and brown sugar. They taste as rich and sunny as a Hawaiian vacation with a pocketful of cash.

Preheat the oven to 350°F. Butter an 8-inch square baking pan and line with parchment paper, leaving a 2-inch overhang on two sides.

In a small saucepan, heat the butter, granulated sugar, and brown sugar over medium heat, whisking occasionally, until the butter is melted and the sugar is mostly dissolved, about 5 minutes. Remove from the heat and stir in the crystallized ginger and minced ginger. Let cool slightly, so as not to scramble the egg in the next step.

Whisk in the egg, rum, lime zest, and vanilla extract. Fold in the flour, salt, and baking soda. Pour the batter into the prepared pan and smooth the top. Sprinkle the nuts evenly over the top and press them lightly to adhere. Bake until just set and a skewer inserted into the center comes out with moist crumbs attached, 18 to 20 minutes. Let cool in the pan on a rack.

To serve, using the parchment paper, transfer the cake to a cutting board and slice into squares. These are best the day they're made, but you can store them in an airtight container for up to 2 days or freeze them for up to a month.

PARSNIP CAKE WITH CREAM CHEESE FROSTING

SERVES 8

CAKE

10 tablespoons (1¼ sticks) unsalted butter, melted and cooled slightly, plus more for greasing the pan

1½ cups (6¾ ounces) all-purpose flour, plus more for dusting the pan

1 tablespoon ground cinnamon

1 tablespoon ground ginger

1½ teaspoons freshly ground cardamom

1½ teaspoons baking powder

¾ teaspoon kosher salt

½ teaspoon baking soda

6 tablespoons packed dark brown sugar

6 tablespoons granulated sugar

2 large eggs

1½ cups peeled, grated parsnips (about 2 medium)

2 tablespoons (1 ounce) peeled, finely grated fresh ginger

2 ounces chopped pecans (about ½ cup), optional

¼ cup whole milk

2 teaspoons pure vanilla extract

FROSTING

4 ounces cream cheese, at room temperature

1 to 2 tablespoons confectioners' sugar

2 tablespoons whole milk, warmed

I know what you're thinking: parsnips? Bear with me. Imagine a carrot cake, but better. In my opinion, parsnips bake up into something even more wonderful. They have a subtle, earthy edge, and a soft sweetness reminiscent of bananas. In fact, after World War II, when imported bananas were scarce in the UK, parsnips were often used as a substitute in baked goods. But this cake is no mere imitator—with ginger, cinnamon, and cardamom, it bakes up moist and flavorful. The cream cheese frosting is not essential, but is always a welcome addition.

Preheat the oven to 350°F. Butter and flour an 8½ by 4½-inch loaf pan.

To prepare the cake, in a medium bowl, whisk together the flour, cinnamon, ground ginger, cardamom, baking powder, salt, and baking soda.

In a large bowl, with a wooden spoon, stir together the butter, brown sugar, and granulated sugar. Add eggs, one at a time, and stir to combine. Stir in the parsnip, fresh ginger, pecans, milk, and vanilla. With a rubber spatula, fold the flour mixture into the butter mixture. Do not overmix the batter. A few streaks of flour aren't a bad thing.

Spoon the batter into the prepared pan and bake until a skewer inserted into the center comes out with moist crumbs attached, about 45 to 50 minutes. Let cool on a rack for 15 minutes, then flip the loaf out of the pan, turn it right side up and let it cool completely.

To prepare the frosting, with a wooden spoon, stir together the cream cheese and confectioners' sugar in a small bowl. Add the warm milk and whisk until smooth. Spread an even layer of frosting on top of the cake.

Store leftovers in an airtight container at room temperature for up to 3 days or frozen (without frosting) for up to 1 month.

GINGERBREAD

SERVES 12

¾ cup (1½ sticks) unsalted butter, melted, plus more for greasing the pan

1¼ cups (5⅝ ounces) all-purpose flour

1¼ cups (5⁵/₁₆ ounces) whole-wheat pastry flour

1 tablespoon ground ginger

2 teaspoons ground cinnamon

1¼ teaspoons baking soda

1 teaspoon freshly ground cardamom

¾ teaspoon kosher salt

¼ teaspoon ground cloves

¼ cup sugar

½ cup honey

1 cup unsulphured molasses

¼ cup (1 ounce) peeled, minced fresh ginger

1 tablespoon finely grated orange zest (from 1 orange)

½ cup sour cream

2 large eggs, lightly beaten

½ cup warm water

Sweetened whipped cream, for serving (optional)

Here it is—the cake of my dreams. My version, inspired by Regan Daley's Black Sticky Gingerbread, has a texture that you're going to want to take a nap on. I have to resist the urge to gently lay my face on it while it's cooling.

This recipe calls for a full cup of molasses. Different brands of molasses vary in intensity, so it's important to consider your tastes before you begin. If you like a deep, dark gingerbread with a strong molasses flavor, go for a dark, unsulphured molasses like Wholesome Sweetener's organic molasses, or Plantation brand organic blackstrap molasses. For a lighter, slightly sweeter touch, use something like Grandma's brand original unsulphured molasses. If you can't decide, try a mix of the two. That's what I do! No matter what, the results are extremely flavorful and moist. I like big, thick slabs served alongside a tall, creamy glass of milk.

Preheat the oven to 325°F. Butter a 9-inch square baking pan. Line the pan with parchment, leaving a 2-inch overhang on two sides. Butter the parchment.

In a medium bowl, whisk together the all-purpose flour, whole-wheat pastry flour, ground ginger, cinnamon, baking soda, cardamom, salt, and cloves. In a large bowl, whisk together the butter, sugar, honey, molasses, fresh ginger, and orange zest. Using a wooden spoon, stir in the sour cream, eggs, and warm water.

Add ½ of the wet mixture to the dry mixture and stir with a wooden spoon until mostly smooth, then add the remaining wet mixture and stir until just combined. Pour the batter into the prepared pan and bake until the cake is set and a toothpick inserted into the center comes out with moist crumbs attached, about 40 to 50 minutes. Let cool completely in the pan on a rack.

To serve, transfer the cake to a cutting board, cut the cake into pieces, and serve with whipped cream. Store the cake well wrapped at room temperature for up to 3 days or frozen for up to 1 month.

HAZELNUT AND OAT COOKIE SANDWICHES

MAKES ABOUT 2 DOZEN SANDWICHES

1 cup (5 ounces) hazelnuts, toasted, skinned, and cooled completely (see page 11)

²/₃ cup sugar, plus more for pressing

1½ cups (5¼ ounces) old-fashioned oats

1 tablespoon ground ginger

¾ teaspoon kosher salt

¼ teaspoon baking powder

½ cup (1 stick) unsalted butter, at room temperature, cut into pieces

1 large egg

⅓ cup (2¼ ounces) crystallized ginger, finely chopped

6 ounces chopped semisweet chocolate (50 to 60 percent cacao), about 1½ cups

These cookies happen to be gluten-free, but I didn't create them that way on purpose. I only started with a vision of what I wanted the cookie to be—a crunchy, buttery, nut cookie sandwich with a dark chocolate filling. The first try turned out okay, but I wanted the ginger, oat, and hazelnut flavors to be stronger. So I got to work on another batch using ¼ cup less flour. But they still weren't sufficiently intense. This happened again and again, with less and less flour, until there happened to be none at all. At that point, the cookies were exactly what I had envisioned. Crisp. Flavorful. Perfect. And naturally gluten-free. Cookies for everyone!

If gluten-sensitivity is an issue, be sure to use gluten-free oats, which have been processed in a wheat-free facility. Also look for gluten-free baking powder, which won't include any wheat starches.

Preheat the oven to 350°F. Line two baking sheets with parchment paper.

In the bowl of a food processor fitted with the metal blade, combine the hazelnuts and sugar and grind until the mixture is uniform and sandy. Be sure to stop before you've made a paste. Add the oats, ground ginger, salt, and baking powder and process until the mixture resembles coarse meal. Add the butter and pulse to combine and then add the egg and pulse until evenly moistened. Transfer the dough to a bowl and stir in the crystallized ginger.

Have ready a small bowl filled with sugar. Scoop the dough in level 1-tablespoon scoops. Roll each scoop into a ball and place it on the prepared sheets about 1½ inches apart. Flatten one of the dough balls with the bottom of a small glass so the glass gets nice and buttery, then dip the glass into the bowl of sugar. Flatten the cookie again so that it gets coated in sugar, then flatten each ball into a 2-inch round, dipping the glass in sugar each time.

Bake the cookies until the edges are light golden, 12 to 15 minutes, rotating the sheets halfway through. Slide the parchment with the cookies gently onto racks to cool completely. Repeat with the remaining dough.

Place the chocolate in a medium bowl over a saucepan of barely simmering water, stirring occasionally, until the chocolate is melted. Make sure that the bottom of the bowl is not touching the water. Alternatively, you could melt the chocolate in the microwave, in 15-second bursts, stirring in between each one. Let the chocolate cool slightly.

Spread about 1 teaspoon of chocolate on the flat side of half of the cookies. Top with the remaining cookies. Let the cookie sandwiches stand at room temperature until the chocolate has set.

Store the cookies in an airtight container at room temperature for up to 3 days or in the freezer for up to a month.

RASPBERRY SHORTCAKE WITH DOUBLE GINGER BISCUITS

SERVES 6

BISCUITS
½ cup cold heavy cream, plus more for brushing

1 large egg

2½ cups (11¼ ounces) all-purpose flour, plus more for the work surface

1 tablespoon baking powder

¼ cup granulated sugar

1 teaspoon ground ginger

½ teaspoon kosher salt

½ cup (1 stick) cold unsalted butter, cut into pieces

¼ cup (1⅝ ounces) crystallized ginger, finely chopped

Sanding sugar, for sprinkling

TO FINISH
12 ounces (2½ cups) fresh raspberries

1 tablespoon granulated sugar

2 cups cold heavy cream

1 to 2 tablespoons confectioners' sugar (optional)

We grew up with raspberry bushes taller than my head lining the back corner of our yard in Connecticut. On those outstanding summer picking days, my dad and I would head out there in the morning and get right to work, the dew wetting our arms and the Japanese beetles humming around our heads. If we could stop ourselves from devouring the lot outside, we would each fill a cereal bowl with berries and eat them with brown sugar and ice-cold, creamy whole milk for breakfast.

These shortcakes remind me of those raspberry mornings of my childhood. The biscuits are best the day they're baked. For perfect shortcakes in no time, freeze the shaped, unbaked squares and bake them from frozen when you're ready. The frozen biscuits may take a minute or two longer to bake, but they'll be just as delicious.

Whisk together the cream and the egg. In a separate large bowl, whisk together the flour, baking powder, sugar, ground ginger, and salt. Using a pastry blender, cut the butter into the flour mixture until it is the texture of coarse meal with some larger pea-size pieces. Add the crystallized ginger and toss to combine.

Mix the cream mixture into the flour mixture with a fork just until a shaggy dough forms. Tip the dough out onto a lightly floured piece of parchment paper and knead it, just 2 or 3 times, to get the mixture to come together. Pat it into a 9 by 6-inch rectangle. With a sharp knife, trim ¼ inch off of each edge, then cut into six squares. Arrange the squares on the sheet about 2 inches apart. Freeze for 20 to 30 minutes. Meanwhile, preheat the oven to 425°F.

Brush the tops of the frozen squares with cream and sprinkle with sanding sugar. Bake until golden brown and puffed slightly, 14 to 16 minutes. Let cool completely on the sheet on a rack. Toss the raspberries with the granulated sugar and let stand until juicy. To serve, whip the 2 cups cream with confectioners' sugar to soft peaks. Split the biscuits and fill them with whipped cream and raspberries.

STICKY APPLE DATE CAKE

SERVES 10

CAKE

10 tablespoons (1¼ sticks) unsalted butter, at room temperature, plus more for greasing the pan

10 ounces (about 20) dates, pitted and chopped (1½ cups)

1 cup water

1 teaspoon baking soda

2 cups (9 ounces) all-purpose flour

1½ teaspoons baking powder

½ teaspoon kosher salt

⅓ cup granulated sugar

2 large eggs, at room temperature

6 tablespoons (1½ ounces) peeled, minced, fresh ginger

2 small sweet-tart apples, such as Pink Lady or Braeburn, peeled, cored and cut into ¼-inch dice (1½ cups)

SAUCE

½ cup packed light brown sugar

6 tablespoons (¾ stick) unsalted butter

1 teaspoon kosher salt

½ cup heavy cream

I'm a sucker for anything date-related. Here I've paired dates with crisp, tart apples and plenty of spicy ginger. Slathered in just the right amount of buttery caramel sauce, this moist cake hits all the right notes. Add a nip of brandy to the sauce for a little something extra. As it cools, the sauce may stiffen up. A little gentle heat will bring it right back, although it makes a tasty frosting as well.

Preheat the oven to 350°F. Butter a 9-inch springform pan. To prepare the cake, bring the dates and the water to a simmer over medium heat in a small saucepan. Cook until the dates start to soften, about 1 minute. Remove from the heat and immediately stir in the baking soda. Set aside to cool.

In a medium bowl, whisk together the flour, baking powder, and salt. In a large bowl, with an electric mixer beat the butter and sugar on medium speed until pale and fluffy, 3 to 4 minutes. Beat in the eggs, one at time, and then add the ginger. Add the flour mixture and beat until just combined. Stir in the date mixture and fold in the apples. Pour the batter into the prepared pan and smooth the top. Bake until a toothpick inserted into the center comes out with moist crumbs attached, 40 to 45 minutes.

Meanwhile, to prepare the sauce, combine the brown sugar, butter, and salt in a medium saucepan. Cook over medium heat until the butter is melted and the sugar dissolves, stirring occasionally, about 3 minutes. Add the heavy cream and bring the mixture to a simmer, then decrease the heat to low. Cook, stirring, until the sauce has thickened, 5 to 7 minutes. Set aside to cool slightly.

Let the cake cool for about 15 minutes, then remove the pan sides and set the cake on a serving plate. Using a toothpick, poke holes all over the cake. Pour half of the warm sauce over the warm cake and let it absorb. Serve the cake warm with the remaining sauce for drizzling. Store leftovers well wrapped at room temperature for up to 3 days.

GINGER NUTS

MAKES ABOUT 4 DOZEN COOKIES

1½ cups (6¾ ounces) all-purpose flour, plus more for the work surface

1½ tablespoons ground ginger

1 teaspoon ground cinnamon

1 teaspoon freshly ground black pepper

½ teaspoon freshly grated nutmeg

½ teaspoon baking soda

½ teaspoon kosher salt

¼ teaspoon ground cloves

⅔ cup packed dark brown sugar

¼ cup (½ stick) unsalted butter, at room temperature

¼ cup unsulphured blackstrap molasses

1 large egg yolk

My love for ginger nuts is legendary in our family. Every time my grandmother introduced me to someone new, she began with the fact that her American granddaughter just couldn't get enough cookies—even when I was well into my twenties! Embarrassing but true.

These snaps have that addictive crunch—the type that interrupts the quiet reading happening in the next room. They're so crunchy that eating them with a cup of tea is not only delicious but also imperative. The baked cookies freeze exceptionally well and are a real treat to find hidden behind the peas long after you've forgotten all about them.

In a medium bowl, whisk together the flour, ginger, cinnamon, pepper, nutmeg, baking soda, salt, and cloves. In a large bowl, with an electric mixer, beat the brown sugar and butter on medium speed until pale and fluffy, 3 to 4 minutes. Add the molasses and egg yolk and beat until combined. Add the flour mixture and beat again until well combined, about 3 minutes. The dough will be wet and pebbly, but it should come together when squeezed.

Scoop the dough onto a piece of plastic wrap and flatten it into an 8-inch disk. Chill the dough until it has firmed up a bit, about 2 hours.

Preheat the oven to 350°F. Line two baking sheets with parchment paper.

On a lightly floured surface, roll the dough to an even ⅛-inch thickness and cut out 2-inch rounds. (Thicker cookies bake up chewy, although equally yummy.) Set the cookies on the prepared baking sheets about ½ inch apart and bake until the tops are dry and the edges begin to darken very slightly, 20 to 25 minutes, rotating the sheets halfway through. Let the cookies cool completely on a rack. Repeat with the remaining dough. Store the cookies in an airtight container at room temperature for up to 5 days or in the freezer for up to a month.

GINGERBREAD PANCAKES

SERVES 6 TO 8 (MAKES ABOUT 16 PANCAKES)

2 cups (9 ounces) all-purpose flour

2½ teaspoons baking powder

2 teaspoons ground ginger

1 teaspoon ground cinnamon

½ teaspoon baking soda

¼ teaspoon ground cloves

½ teaspoon kosher salt

1⅓ cups buttermilk

½ cup unsulphured molasses

3 tablespoons unsalted butter, melted and cooled slightly, plus more for greasing the skillet

2 teaspoons peeled finely grated fresh ginger

2 large eggs

I didn't realize that pancake batter could come from anything but a carton until I was in college. Aunt Jemima was practically a member of our family when I was growing up. These gingerbread pancakes are a far cry from the pancakes of my childhood. They're puffy and delicately spiced with both fresh and dried ground ginger. With plenty of molasses, and all that spice, they're tasty enough to eat straight out of the skillet with an extra pat of butter. Or, instead of maple syrup, serve them with a bit of applesauce for a luscious and fresh pairing.

Preheat the oven to 200°F. Set a baking sheet in the oven.

In a medium bowl, whisk together the flour, baking powder, ground ginger, cinnamon, baking soda, cloves, and salt. In a second medium bowl, whisk together the buttermilk, molasses, butter, fresh ginger, and eggs. Add the egg mixture to the flour mixture and whisk again just until combined. Don't overmix the batter. The batter should be slightly lumpy.

Melt a pat of butter in a large nonstick skillet over medium-high heat. Working in batches, drop about ¼ cup of batter into the skillet to form each pancake. Cook until small bubbles appear on the surface of the pancake, 3 to 4 minutes. Flip the pancakes and cook until risen and golden brown, adjusting the heat as needed, 2 to 5 minutes more.

Set the finished pancakes on the baking sheet and keep warm in the oven, or just gobble them up as you go. Repeat with more butter and remaining batter, wiping the skillet clean with a paper towel between batches.

CHOCOLATE-DIPPED GINGER MACAROONS

MAKES ABOUT 3½ DOZEN COOKIES

4 large egg whites

⅔ cup sugar

½ teaspoon kosher salt

4 cups (12 ounces) unsweetened shredded coconut

¼ cup (1⅝ ounces) crystallized ginger, finely chopped

8 ounces chopped bittersweet chocolate (60 to 70 percent cacao), about 2 cups

When I was small, scraping the flesh out of fresh coconut halves was one of my favorite kitchen jobs. Tikiri, my grandmother's cook, would attach a small, hand-operated grater to the edge of the countertop and let me go at it. My head barely cleared the edge of the counter, yet I guided the coconut half with one tiny hand and cranked the scraper with the other. It probably took me about five times longer than it would have taken Tikiri. But I'm sure she could see the huge grin that lit up my face as the milky white coconut flaked onto the counter.

These days I rarely find my kitchen full of fresh coconuts. Too bad. But store-bought shredded coconut is great. I prefer to use unsweetened shredded coconut for most of my baking. Without the added sugar, the coconut flavor really shines. These coconut macaroons, not to be confused with French macarons, are also flavored with spicy-sweet crystallized ginger. The result is a pure tropical treat.

Preheat the oven to 350°F. Line two baking sheets with parchment paper.

In a large bowl, whisk together the egg whites, sugar, and salt. Stir in the coconut and ginger. Drop the dough in packed 1-tablespoon scoops about 1 inch apart on the prepared baking sheets. Bake until golden, 18 to 22 minutes, rotating the sheets halfway through. Let cool on the sheets.

Place the chocolate in a medium bowl over a pot of barely simmering water, stirring occasionally, until the chocolate is melted. Make sure that the bottom of the bowl is not touching the water. Alternatively, you could melt the chocolate in the microwave, in 15-second bursts, stirring in between each one.

Dip half of each cookie in the chocolate and return to the sheet. Chill 10 minutes to set the chocolate.

Store the macaroons in an airtight container in the fridge for up to 5 days or in the freezer for up to a month.

GINGERED STRAWBERRY RHUBARB PIE

SERVES 10

PASTRY

3 cups (13½ ounces) all-purpose flour, plus more for the work surface and the rolling pin

2 tablespoons granulated sugar

¾ teaspoon kosher salt

1 cup plus 2 tablespoons (2¼ sticks) cold unsalted butter, cut into cubes

8 to 10 tablespoons ice water

FILLING

2 pounds fresh strawberries, hulled and quartered (about 6 cups)

½ cup granulated sugar

1 pound rhubarb, trimmed and cut into ¼-inch slices (about 3½ cups)

½ cup packed dark brown sugar

¼ cup cornstarch

1 teaspoons finely grated lime zest plus 1 tablespoon juice (from 1 lime)

2 teaspoons peeled, minced fresh ginger

TO FINISH

1 large egg yolk

2 teaspoons water

Sanding sugar, for sprinkling

1 tablespoons butter, cut into small pieces

A strawberry pie is best undertaken when the season is right and the berries are fragrant and juicy. But juicy berries can lead to an even juicier pie, which isn't always a good thing. After several delicious but drippy tests of this beauty, I remembered a trick from Christine Ferber, France's jam genius, for creating extra-flavorful fruit jams: macerate the fruit before cooking. To macerate fruit is to toss it with sugar and let it stand to remove extra liquid and intensify the flavor. I gave it a shot, *et voilà!*—extra juice ran off before the berries went into the pie, so the set was much more sliceable and the strawberry flavor that much more concentrated. *Merci*, Christine! If your berries aren't the very juiciest, feel free to omit this step.

To prepare the pastry, whisk together the flour, granulated sugar, and salt in a large bowl. Cut the butter in with a pastry blender or two knives until the mixture resembles coarse meal with a few pea-size pieces. Add 8 tablespoons water and stir with a fork until a shaggy dough starts to form. Add 1 or 2 more tablespoons of water if you need to, but stop before the dough gets too wet. It should just hold together when you squeeze it in your hand. Gather the dough into a rough ball in the bowl with your hands. Halve the dough and wrap each piece in plastic wrap. Flatten and shape them into two 6-inch disks. Refrigerate until cold, about 2 hours or up to 2 days. Alternatively, freeze the dough, well wrapped, for up to 1 month.

Have ready a 9½-inch glass pie plate that is 1¾ inches deep.

On a lightly floured surface, with a lightly floured rolling pin, roll one disk of pastry out to about a 13-inch circle, ⅛ inch thick. Carefully set the dough in the pie plate, easing it into the bottom and sides, and trim off excess dough, leaving a ½-inch overhang to work with. On a lightly floured piece of parchment, roll the second disk out to a 13-inch circle. Using a fluted pastry wheel, cut

CONTINUED

the circle into 1-inch strips. Chill the bottom crust and the strips for at least 1 hour.

Preheat the oven to 400°F. Set a colander over a large bowl. Line a rimmed baking sheet with aluminum foil.

Meanwhile, to prepare the filling, toss the strawberries with 2 tablespoons of the sugar in the colander. Let them stand, stirring occasionally, until they have released some of their juice and softened slightly, about 45 minutes. (Save that delicious juice for adding to seltzer or drizzling over yogurt.)

In a large bowl, combine the strawberries, rhubarb, brown sugar, cornstarch, lime zest and juice, ginger, and the remaining 6 tablespoons of granulated sugar. Fill the chilled pastry bottom with the strawberry mixture.

Top the pie evenly with five of the pastry strips. Fold them into a lattice pattern. To do this, think of the strips as numbered 1 to 5. Fold strips 2 and 4 halfway over themselves and lay another pastry strip (6) in the opposite direction on top of the pie. Unfold strips 2 and 4 over 6. Then fold back strips 1, 3, and 5 back and slip another strip (7) over the top of the pie. Fold strips 1, 3, and 5 back over strip 7. Continue with this pattern until you've used all of the strips evenly over the top. Trim the strips to the same length as the overhang from the bottom crust. Fold the overhang over to create an even rim and crimp the edges.

In a small bowl, make an egg wash by whisking the egg yolk with the 2 teaspoons water. Brush the egg wash evenly over the top of the pie. Sprinkle with sanding sugar. Dot the exposed filling with the butter.

Set the pie on the prepared baking sheet and bake for 30 minutes. Decrease the heat to 375°F and continue to bake until the crust is deep golden brown and the filling is bubbling, about 30 minutes.

Cool completely on a rack before serving. Although runny, the pie is still pretty delicious if you can't wait. Store leftovers, well wrapped, in the fridge for up to 2 days. Leftovers start to get soft after the first day but I don't know anyone who doesn't enjoy a fruity slice of pie for breakfast.

GRAPEFRUIT CURD AND POPPY SEED PIE

SERVES 10

PASTRY

1½ cups (6¾ ounces) all-purpose flour, plus more for the work surface and the rolling pin

¼ cup confectioners' sugar

¼ cup packed light brown sugar

4 teaspoons poppy seeds

½ teaspoon kosher salt

10 tablespoons (1¼ sticks) cold unsalted butter, cut into small pieces

2 large egg yolks, lightly beaten

1 tablespoon ice water, if necessary

1 large egg white, lightly beaten

CURD

8 large egg yolks

½ cup granulated sugar

2 tablespoons cornstarch

⅛ teaspoon kosher salt

1¼ cups freshly squeezed grapefruit juice (from 2 to 3 grapefruits)

1 tablespoon grated grapefruit zest (from 1 grapefruit)

2 tablespoons freshly squeezed lemon juice (from 1 lemon)

2 tablespoons (1 ounce) peeled, finely grated fresh ginger

¼ cup (½ stick) unsalted butter

Eating shortbread cookies with a swipe of fresh citrus curd is one of life's great pleasures, and the inspiration for this pie. The buttery poppy-studded base combined with the tangy, creamy filling is just heavenly. Truth be told, the parts are pretty good on their own, too. Make the curd alone and you'll be rewarded with a delicious topping for biscuits and scones, a tangy filling for cakes, or even an alternative to syrup on pancakes. The possibilities are endless.

To prepare the crust, add the flour, confectioners' sugar, brown sugar, poppy seeds, and salt to the bowl of a food processor fitted with the metal blade and pulse to combine. Add the butter and pulse until the mixture resembles coarse meal. Add the egg yolks and pulse just until the mixture is evenly moistened. Add the water if necessary. Tip the dough onto a piece of plastic wrap. Using the sides of the plastic wrap, ease the mound into a ball, wrap it up, and flatten it into a 6-inch disk. Refrigerate until cold, about 2 hours or up to 2 days. Alternatively, freeze the dough, well wrapped, for up to 1 month.

Preheat the oven to 350°F. Have ready a 9-inch fluted tart pan with a removable bottom.

On a lightly floured surface, with a lightly floured rolling pin, roll the dough out to an 11-inch circle. Ease the dough into the tart pan, gently pressing in the edges, then run a rolling pin over the top to trim the edges. Refrigerate for at least 30 minutes or freeze for 15 minutes. Line the cold pastry with parchment paper and fill with pie weights or dried beans. Place the lined tart pan on a baking sheet and bake until set and dry, about 20 minutes. Carefully lift the parchment and the weights to peek underneath and check. Remove the parchment and the weights and continue to bake the crust until light golden brown and crisp, 15 to 18 minutes more. Immediately brush the inside bottom and sides of the crust with a light coat of the egg white. Let cool completely on a rack.

TO FINISH

1½ cups heavy cream

1 to 2 tablespoons confectioners' sugar

1 teaspoon poppy seeds, for sprinkling

Set a fine-mesh sieve over a large bowl.

To prepare the curd, whisk together the egg yolks, granulated sugar, cornstarch, and salt in a medium saucepan. Whisk in the grapefruit juice, grapefruit zest, lemon juice, and ginger. Cook over medium-low heat, stirring with a wooden spoon, until the mixture begins to thicken, 4 to 5 minutes. Once it comes to a low boil, cook it, stirring constantly, for another minute. Immediately strain the curd through the sieve into the bowl. Whisk in the butter. Let cool until just warm, then pour into the baked crust. Cover with plastic wrap and chill until set, at least 2 hours.

To serve, whip the cream and confectioners' sugar to soft peaks. Top the tart with the whipped cream and sprinkle with poppy seeds. Store leftovers, well wrapped, in the fridge for up to 1 day.

savory herbs
& spices

We all know what cinnamon and nutmeg can do for desserts. These and the other spices I've written about so far are common in the baker's pantry for good reason. So many classic desserts depend on them. But what about all the other treasures on the spice rack? Many of the spices and herbs more commonly used as savory accents have a place in the sweet kitchen, too. Here are a few of my favorites.

BAY LEAVES

These are the leaves of an evergreen tree, also known as sweet bay or bay laurel, and are most commonly used to flavor long-cooking soups and stews. I find that they add a subtle warmth, with notes of both citrus and allspice, to creamy desserts, like pudding and custards. For these dishes, which don't require hours of simmering, the fresh leaves are much better than dried. Their flavor infuses very quickly and has a brighter taste. Leftover fresh leaves can be used in any dish that calls for dried leaves. Look for them in your supermarket where the fresh herbs are sold.

FENNEL SEED AND ANISE SEED

Some say that fennel seed should be reserved for savory dishes and anise seed, a member of the parsley family, is better for sweet. I say pish posh to that. Both have a distinct licorice flavor and both are lovely in desserts. Even as someone who loathes licorice candy, I think that fennel and anise can be the perfect addition to a crunchy biscotti, a buttery lemon cookie, or even a simple apple pie. Just the right amount adds a refreshing, subtle sweetness. The name "fennel" comes from the Latin word *foeniculum,* which means "fragrant hay," an inviting and appropriate description.

LAVENDER

I encourage you to think beyond your linens and consider lavender for your next baking project. The buds of this gorgeous flowering plant, part of the mint family, add a pleasant herbal, floral essence to desserts. I especially love lavender mixed with blackberries, peaches, and strawberries. And it's good in savory preparations, too. Grind up lavender with a little salt and sprinkle it on your next chicken or steak for an unexpected, tasty treat.

SAFFRON

The beautiful orange threads that we call saffron are stigmas of saffron crocuses. Saffron is the most expensive spice by weight. Understandably so, as the bulbs must be replanted yearly and hand pollinated. Like the vanilla orchid, the saffron crocus only blooms for a day, so the stigmas must be harvested immediately and then dried. It grows in Iran, Spain, India, Greece, Morocco, and Italy. Legend has it that Cleopatra liked to bathe in it. I just use it to flavor custards, puddings, and breads.

ALLSPICE

Allspice is the fruit of an evergreen tree from the myrtle family native to the Caribbean. Allspice berries are picked before fully ripe. Then, to release the flavor, the berries are packed in bags to sweat. After they are dried, they begin to look like the reddish brown orbs we're familiar with. The berries have a flavor reminiscent of cinnamon, nutmeg, and cloves, which is probably how allspice earned its name. Use it whole, simmered and steeped, to add flavor to any preparation that calls for warm spices, or grind the whole berries in a spice grinder.

CARAWAY

Despite its more commonly known application in rye bread, caraway is an excellent addition to desserts, too. It's especially wonderful alongside apples and pears, or swirled into sweet cheese. Caraway seeds are actually the fruit of a biennial plant in the carrot family. Native to Central Europe, Asia, and North Africa, caraway has been used medicinally for centuries. Some say the little seeds can even improve the appetite—as if I need any help in that department.

APPLE DANISH WITH CARAWAY CREAM

SERVES 10

PASTRY

1½ cups (6¾ ounces) bread flour, plus more for the work surface and the rolling pin

2 tablespoons granulated sugar

2 teaspoons active dry yeast

¾ teaspoon kosher salt

¾ cup plus 2 tablespoons (1¾ sticks) cold, unsalted butter, cut into ¼-inch pieces

1 large egg

¼ cup cold whole milk

2 tablespoons water

FILLING

¼ cup (½ stick) unsalted butter

3 tablespoons packed dark brown sugar

½ teaspoon ground cinnamon

Pinch of kosher salt

4 medium sweet and tart apples, such as Braeburn (about 6 ounces each), peeled, cored, and thinly sliced

6 ounces cream cheese, at room temperature

¼ cup granulated sugar

1 egg yolk

2 teaspoons cornstarch

¾ teaspoon caraway seeds

TO FINISH

1 egg yolk

2 teaspoons water

Pearl sugar, for sprinkling (optional)

Apples and caraway you know. Have you ever had them folded together and tucked into a flaky pastry alongside a sweet cream cheese filling? The light-citrus, almost anise-like flavor of the caraway seeds works so well with all of that rich cream and butter.

A true Danish pastry starts with an enriched, yeasted dough wrapped and folded around a butter block. This version is made using a shortcut method, where the butter is simply tossed in with the yeast and flour and rolled a few times. The results are miraculous. Chewy, crisp Danish dough made much simpler.

You can use the remaining 2 tablespoons of cream cheese, whisked with a little milk and confectioners' sugar, to a make a light glaze for the finished pastry. She's a beaut without it, but sometimes a situation may call for a little extra flair.

To prepare the pastry, combine the flour, granulated sugar, yeast, and salt in a large bowl. Add the butter and toss to combine. (Make sure the butter pieces are truly ¼ inch or even a little smaller.) In a small bowl, whisk together the egg, milk, and water. Add the egg mixture to the flour mixture and, using a rubber spatula, fold the mixture until it is evenly moistened. Take care not to incorporate the butter. You want those butter pieces to stay whole. Turn the dough out onto a piece of plastic wrap, shape into a small rectangle, and wrap well. Chill for at least 3 hours, and up to overnight.

On a lightly floured surface, let the dough warm up for a minute or so. With a lightly floured rolling pin, roll the dough to a rectangle that's about 8 by 15 inches, with a short side facing you. Fold the dough into thirds like a letter. (Fold the top third down and the bottom third up over the top third.) Use a bench scraper to help lift and fold the dough if necessary. At this point, the dough will be rough and shaggy with visible butter pieces. As you roll

CONTINUED

and fold the dough it will come together. Rotate the dough so the folded edge is to the left. Repeat this process two more times, dusting the work surface, your hands, and the rolling pin with flour as necessary. Wrap the dough with plastic wrap and refrigerate for at least 30 minutes. Repeat the entire process one more time for a grand total of six turns. Wrap the dough and refrigerate it for at least 6 hours, or up to overnight. If the dough starts to fight you and become difficult to roll at any point along the way, just pop it in the fridge for an extra rest.

To prepare the apple filling, melt the butter over medium heat in a large skillet. Add the brown sugar, cinnamon, and salt and stir to combine with a heatproof rubber spatula. Add the apples and cook, gently stirring occasionally, until the apples are tender, all the juices have evaporated, and the sauce is lightly caramelized, 8 to 10 minutes. Tip the apple mixture onto a plate to cool it to room temperature, or chill the filling until you're ready to use it.

In a small bowl, stir together the cream cheese and the granulated sugar until smooth. Stir in the egg yolk, cornstarch, and caraway seeds. Chill until ready to assemble.

On a lightly floured piece of parchment, roll the dough into a 10 by 14-inch rectangle, with a short side facing you. With a bench scraper or the backside of a knife, very lightly mark off a 3-inch section lengthwise down the center of the dough. Don't cut through the dough, but make a guide for yourself. Next, cut 1-inch strips, perpendicular to the lengthwise guidelines, on either side of the 3-inch section. (You will fold these strips over later to create a braided pattern.)

In a small bowl, make an egg wash by whisking together the egg yolk and the 2 teaspoons water. Spread the cream cheese mixture down the center of the pastry, leaving a small border on all sides. Top evenly with the apple mixture. Very lightly, brush a 1-inch border of the pastry with the egg wash. Cover the egg wash with plastic wrap and set it aside.

Start by folding up the top and bottom ends to create a barrier for the filling. Next, fold each strip over the filling, alternating from left to right and moving toward the bottom. Using the parchment, move the filled pastry onto a rimmed baking sheet.

Let the dough stand until puffed. Note the thickness of the strips when you first set it aside and use their growth as a guide. It's ready when it looks puffy and the dough bounces back slowly when pressed lightly. If it bounces back too fast, it hasn't risen enough—and if it doesn't bounce back at all, it's gone too far.

While the dough is rising, preheat the oven to 400°F.

Gently brush the top and sides of the pastry with the egg wash and sprinkle with pearl sugar. Bake until the pastry is golden brown and puffed, 18 to 22 minutes. Let cool slightly on the sheet.

When ready to serve, a serrated knife works well for slicing. This Danish is best the day it's made but leftovers can be stored at room temperature for up to 2 days.

PROFITEROLES WITH COCONUT ALLSPICE ICE CREAM AND HOT FUDGE

**6 TO 9 SERVINGS
(2 TO 3 PROFITEROLES
PER PERSON)**

ICE CREAM

1½ cups heavy cream

1¼ cups milk

1½ cups (4½ ounces) unsweetened large-flake shredded coconut, toasted (see page 10)

1 tablespoon whole allspice berries, crushed lightly

6 large egg yolks

½ cup sugar

¼ teaspoon kosher salt

1 cup coconut milk

PUFFS

6 tablespoons (¾ stick) unsalted butter, cut into small pieces

2 teaspoons sugar

½ teaspoon kosher salt

¾ cup water

¾ cup (3⅜ ounces) all-purpose flour

3 large eggs

SAUCE

¾ cup coconut milk

½ teaspoon kosher salt

6 ounces bittersweet chocolate (60 to 70 percent cacao), chopped (about 1½ cups)

I was eight when my parents took our family to Paris for a vacation. In retrospect, I'm ashamed that I didn't care more about the *Mona Lisa* or the Eiffel Tower. I gave those landmarks a passing nod, but there was only one thing in Paris that really wowed me: éclairs. Each morning we would pop down to the local *patisserie*, wait in a chaotic line of people clamoring to make their orders heard, and choose treats. Every day I chose an éclair. I'd tear into it right on the sidewalk, custard sloppily dropping onto my hightops. That is *la vie en rose* to me.

These adorable ice cream–stuffed profiteroles are inspired by those Paris éclairs. The coconut and allspice give the French classic some decidedly tropical flair. You can make the ice cream up to a week in advance.

To prepare the ice cream, whisk together the cream, milk, 1 cup of the coconut, and the allspice in a medium saucepan. Bring to a simmer over medium-high heat, remove from the heat, cover, and set aside to infuse for at least 1 hour.

In a medium bowl, whisk together the yolks, sugar, and salt. Add the cream mixture to the yolk mixture and whisk until well-combined. Return the mixture to the pan and cook over medium-low heat, stirring constantly with a wooden spoon, until it is just thick enough to coat the back of a wooden spoon, 4 to 6 minutes. It's important not to let the mixture come to a boil or it will curdle. For this reason, it's better to take the mixture off the heat too early rather than too late.

Have a large bowl of ice water ready.

Pour the coconut milk into a medium bowl and set a fine-mesh sieve over the bowl. Strain the cream mixture through the sieve, pressing the solids to extract the most liquid. Discard the solids. Set the bowl into the larger

CONTINUED

bowl of ice water. Stir occasionally with a wooden spoon until the mixture is completely chilled and very thick. Alternatively, cover well with plastic wrap and chill until very cold, at least 12 hours.

Freeze in an ice cream maker according to the manufacturer's instructions. Pour the ice cream into a freezer-proof container and freeze completely. You should have about a quart of ice cream.

Preheat the oven to 450°F. Line two baking sheets with parchment paper.

To prepare the puffs, bring the butter, sugar, salt, and water to a simmer over medium heat in a medium saucepan, stirring with a wooden spoon to encourage the butter to melt. As soon as it comes to a boil, add the flour, stirring constantly, until the dough forms a ball and pulls away from the sides of the pan, about 1 minute. Remove the pan from the heat and let the mixture cool for 3 to 4 minutes, stirring the dough occasionally. (You don't want the eggs to scramble in the next step.)

Add the eggs, one at a time, stirring vigorously between each addition with a wooden spoon. The dough will break apart and slide around in the pot before it comes back together. Drop the dough in 2-tablespoon scoops about 3 inches apart on the prepared sheets. With an offset spatula, shape the scoops into neat, rounded mounds and flatten any points. Bake until deep golden brown and puffed, rotating the sheets halfway through, 22 to 26 minutes. Let cool completely on a rack.

To prepare the sauce, in a small saucepan, bring the coconut milk and salt to a simmer over medium heat. Remove from the heat and stir in the chocolate. Let the mixture stand for 1 minute and then whisk to make a smooth sauce.

Just before assembling, let the ice cream stand at room temperature for 5 minutes to soften slightly. To assemble, slice off the top third of each puff, fill each with a small scoop of ice cream, replace the top, drizzle with some chocolate sauce, and sprinkle with some of the remaining coconut. Filled profiteroles are best enjoyed immediately.

BAY LEAF RICE PUDDING

SERVES 4 TO 6

4 cups whole milk

2½ ounces sushi rice (about ⅓ cup plus 1 tablespoon)

⅓ cup packed light brown sugar

¼ teaspoon kosher salt

10 fresh bay leaves, each crushed lightly but not broken

2 large egg yolks

¼ cup dried currants

⅛ teaspoon finely grated lemon zest (from 1 lemon)

In Sri Lanka, to say "we're having rice for lunch" doesn't simply imply a pile of white grain. The word *rice* means a full meal of curries, sambols, and chutneys. It means we're going to sit at the table together and catch up. It means we're going to laugh with our mouths full. I've always loved that. Rice means food, family, and comfort.

My second-favorite combination of rice and comfort is rice pudding. The crushed fresh bay leaves add a welcome hint of citrus, mint, and nutmeg to the custard. No one will be able to guess what you've added to the pudding, but they'll know it's one of the best rice puddings they've ever had.

Sushi rice, a short-grain variety, releases just the right amount of starch to thicken the custard nicely. Either Arborio or carnaroli rice would make a fine substitute.

In a large saucepan, combine the milk, rice, brown sugar, salt, and bay leaves. Bring the mixture to a boil over medium-high heat, stirring often with a wooden spoon to keep the rice from sticking to the bottom of the pot. Immediately decrease the heat to medium to maintain a low simmer and cook, stirring occasionally, until the rice is tender, 10 to 15 minutes. Remove from the heat and discard the bay leaves.

Whisk the egg yolks in a medium bowl. Add about ½ cup of the hot milk mixture to the yolks while whisking. Repeat this process until most of the hot milk mixture is in the bowl. Pour the yolk mixture back into the pot and set it over low heat. Cook, stirring, until the pudding has thickened slightly, about 1 minute. Pour the pudding into to a clean bowl and stir in the currants and lemon zest. Let the pudding cool slightly. It will thicken up a little more as it sits.

Serve warm or cover and chill until ready to serve. Keep leftovers in an airtight container in the fridge for up to 3 days.

PEAR TARTE TATIN WITH ANISE SEED CARAMEL

SERVES 8

PASTRY

1½ cups (6¾ ounces) all-purpose flour, plus more for the work surface and the rolling pin

½ teaspoon kosher salt

½ cup (1 stick) cold unsalted butter, cut into pieces

3 to 5 tablespoons ice water

PEARS

6 tablespoons (¾ stick) unsalted butter

⅓ cup sugar

½ teaspoon anise seed

Pinch of kosher salt

4 medium-ripe Bosc pears (about 7 ounces each), peeled, cored, and cut into sixths

TO FINISH

Crème fraîche or vanilla ice cream, for serving

If you have trepidations about piecrust, let this tarte tatin ease your mind. From France, tarte tatin is a simple upside-down caramelized fruit tart. No matter what you do, however it slumps and curves, and whatever bubbles up, the dessert is always beautiful. Rustic and lovely. Legend has it that tarte tatin was born from a mistake when Mme. Fanny Tatin forgot to line her apple tart with pastry. She threw the pastry on top, flipped the tart over, and created a classic. I make my version with succulent pears and a bit of anise seed to flavor the bittersweet caramel. Serve it with a traditional dollop of crème fraîche.

To prepare the dough, whisk together the flour and salt in a large bowl. Cut the butter in with a pastry blender or two knives until the mixture resembles coarse meal with a few pea-size pieces. Add 3 tablespoons ice water and stir with a fork until a shaggy dough forms. Add 1 to 2 more tablespoons water if necessary, but stop before the dough gets too wet. It should just hold together when you squeeze it in your hand. Gather the dough into a rough ball in the bowl with your hands. Set the dough on a piece of plastic wrap, wrap it up, and flatten it into a 6-inch disk. Refrigerate until cold, about 2 hours or up to 2 days. Alternatively, freeze the dough, well wrapped, for up to 1 month.

Preheat the oven to 400°F.

On a lightly floured surface, with a lightly floured rolling pin, roll the dough out to a 10-inch circle. Set the pastry on a plate, cover with plastic wrap, and chill until the pears are ready.

To prepare the pears, melt the butter in a 10-inch ovenproof skillet. Sprinkle the sugar evenly over the melted butter and cook over medium until the mixture begins to turn amber, swirling the pan occasionally, about 2 minutes. (Don't worry if the mixture separates. Once you add the pears it will smooth out again.) Remove from the heat,

CONTINUED

sprinkle the anise seeds and salt evenly over the caramel, and carefully top with the pears. Return to the heat and cook until the caramel turns a deep amber, occasionally stirring and flipping the pears gently with a heat proof rubber spatula, 10 to 12 minutes. The mixture should be simmering, but not too vigorously, or the caramel may break. Adjust the heat as necessary. Take care not to smash the pears.

Remove the skillet from the heat. If you like, you can use a fork and the spatula to carefully rearrange the pears into a pretty pattern. I think it looks just as lovely when the pears are haphazardly strewn about. Top with the round of pastry, tucking the edges in with the spatula. Using a paring knife, cut 4 small slits in the pastry. Bake until the top is golden brown and the caramel is bubbling, 24 to 28 minutes. Let cool on a rack for 5 minutes. (Be sure to wrap the skillet handle with a towel for safety.)

Run a knife around the edge to loosen any pears that might be stuck. Top the skillet with an overturned plate that is at least 1 inch larger than the skillet. Quickly flip the skillet so that the tart is right-side-up on the plate. Rearrange any pears that have fallen out of place and scrape any caramel from the skillet onto the tart.

Serve warm topped with a dollop of crème fraîche or a scoop of vanilla ice cream. Store leftovers well wrapped in the fridge for up to 2 days.

FIG AND FENNEL SEED BISCOTTI

MAKES ABOUT 3 DOZEN COOKIES

2¼ cups (10⅛ ounces) all-purpose flour

½ cup granulated sugar

¼ cup packed light brown sugar

2 teaspoons baking powder

2 teaspoons fennel seeds, chopped

½ teaspoon kosher salt

5 ounces dried Calimyrna figs, stemmed and finely chopped (about 1 cup)

4 ounces walnuts, chopped (about 1 cup)

3 large eggs, lightly beaten

Sanding sugar, for sprinkling (optional)

While I usually pass on licorice, I love fennel. Twizzlers should make a fennel flavor. In this recipe, its grassy essence is lovely with the wine-like sweetness of the dried figs and warm, toasty walnuts.

To make chopping fennel seeds a little easier, use a slightly damp cutting board and knife. The moisture keeps the seeds in place while you're working.

Preheat the oven to 350°F. Line a baking sheet with parchment paper.

In a large bowl, whisk together the flour, granulated sugar, brown sugar, baking powder, fennel seeds, and salt. Stir in the figs and walnuts. With an electric mixer, beat in the eggs on medium speed until the dough is evenly moistened, 1 to 3 minutes. Gather the dough into a ball.

Halve the dough and using slightly wet hands, roll each half into a 10-inch log. Set the logs on the prepared baking sheet at least 2 inches apart. Flatten each log to 2½ inches wide. Sprinkle the tops with sanding sugar. Bake until golden brown and puffed and a toothpick inserted into the center of one log comes out clean, 25 to 30 minutes. The top will look dry and cracked. Let the logs sit on the sheet on a rack until cool enough to handle. Decrease the oven temperature to 325°F.

Set one of the logs onto a cutting board. With a serrated knife, cut it into ¼-inch slices. Arrange the slices, cut side down, on the prepared baking sheets. Repeat with the remaining log. The cookies won't spread at this point, so they can be set close together. Bake until the cookies are lightly browned and beginning to crisp, rotating the sheets halfway through, 20 to 25 minutes. Transfer the cookies to racks to cool completely.

Store the cookies in an airtight container at room temperature for up to 5 days or in the freezer for up to a month.

SAFFRON CURRANT BRAID

MAKES 1 LOAF

¼ cup (½ stick) unsalted butter, at room temperature, cut into ½-inch pieces, plus more for greasing the pan

½ cup whole milk

⅛ teaspoon saffron threads, crushed

1 large egg

2 cups bread flour (9 ounces) plus 2 tablespoons, if necessary

2½ ounces (½ cup) dried currants

¼ cup granulated sugar

1½ teaspoons active dry yeast

½ teaspoon kosher salt

TO FINISH

1 large egg yolk

2 teaspoons water

Pearl sugar, for sprinkling (optional)

My friend Amy, who lives in Sweden, loves *lussekatter*, the delightful saffron-scented, S-shaped buns Swedes make each December thirteenth to celebrate Saint Lucia. On one recent February visit, I suggested we make some, but Amy, a stickler for tradition, thought it would be strange to bake them out of season. I admire her commitment. This saffron currant bread is inspired by *lussekatter* and is equally delicious. I'm hoping that since I'm not Swedish, and the loaves are not the traditional form, I've given Amy a way to bake a soft, saffron-infused treat all year round without breaking any rules.

I could eat an entire loaf of this bread by myself. I find that slices are as wonderful toasted up with butter and jam as they are on either side of a savory sandwich.

———————————————————

Lightly butter a large bowl.

To prepare the dough, in a small saucepan, bring the milk and saffron just to a boil over medium heat. Watch closely to ensure that the milk doesn't boil over. Pour the mixture into a 1-cup liquid measuring cup and top it off with enough water to bring the level back to ½ cup. Let it cool to 105°F to 110°F. (It should be warm to the touch but not too hot.) Add the whole egg and stir to combine.

In the bowl of a stand mixer fitted with the paddle attachment, or in a large bowl with a wooden spoon, combine the flour, currants, sugar, yeast, and salt on low speed. Add the milk mixture and mix just until combined.

Switch to the dough hook and knead the dough on low speed, about 3 minutes. Or, knead it by hand for about 6 minutes. Add the butter, a piece or two at a time. It may look like it's not getting in there but don't worry, it will; just keep adding and kneading. (You might have to stop the mixer and knead the butter in with your hands for a minute to get it started.) Once incorporated, increase the

CONTINUED

speed to medium and knead the dough for another few minutes until it is smooth and elastic. Or tip the dough onto a work surface and knead by hand until smooth. During this stage you can add a bit more flour if the dough is too wet, but don't add more than 2 tablespoons. The dough should just pull away from the sides of the bowl.

Put the dough in the prepared buttered bowl, fold it in on itself at 12, 3, 6, and 9 o'clock, flip it over, cover it with plastic wrap, and set aside in a warm, draft-free place to double in size. This could take 30 minutes or 2 hours, depending on how warm your house is. It's best to just keep an eye on it and watch the dough rather than the clock.

Tip the dough out onto a work surface. You shouldn't need flour at this point. Gently press out the air and fold the dough in on itself at 12, 3, 6, and 9 o'clock. Turn it over and pop it back in the buttered bowl for another rise.

Butter a 4½ by 8½-inch loaf pan.

Once the dough has almost doubled again, tip it onto a work surface. Divide the dough into 3 equal pieces. Stretch and roll each piece into an even 10-inch rope. Pinch the ropes together at one end, braid them tightly, and pinch them at the ends to seal. Place the braid in the prepared loaf pan. Cover it lightly with plastic wrap.

Meanwhile, preheat the oven to 375°F.

In a small bowl, make an egg wash by whisking the egg yolk with the water, and gently brush over the top of the loaf. Sprinkle the top with pearl sugar. Bake until deep golden brown and set, 24 to 28 minutes. Tent the bread with aluminum foil if it is getting too dark. Let cool in the pan on a rack for 20 minutes, then tip the loaf out of the pan and turn right-side-up to cool completely.

Store the bread, well wrapped, at room temperature for up to 3 days or frozen for up to a month.

SUMMER STONE-FRUIT SKILLET CAKE

SERVES 8

6 tablespoons (¾ stick) unsalted butter, at room temperature, plus more for greasing the skillet

1 cup (4½ ounces) all-purpose flour

½ cup (2¼ ounces) fine-ground yellow cornmeal

1¼ teaspoons baking powder

¾ teaspoon anise seed, chopped

½ teaspoon kosher salt

¼ teaspoon baking soda

½ cup plus 1 tablespoon sugar

2 large eggs, at room temperature

1 teaspoon pure vanilla extract

½ cup sour cream, at room temperature

2 small apricots (about 2 to 3 ounces each), pitted and thinly sliced

2 small plums (about 3 to 4 ounces each), pitted and thinly sliced

There is something so homey about a cake served in a skillet. It's casual and inviting—the kind of thing you and your guests could share without plates, if the mood struck you. The anise seed in this recipe adds a subtle, sweet, and spicy warmth without overpowering the fruit. Top the cake with a little ice cream for an easy and perfect summer dessert.

Just like with fennel seed, a damp cutting board and knife make chopping the anise seed much simpler.

Preheat the oven to 350°F. Butter a 10-inch ovenproof skillet.

In a small bowl, whisk together the flour, cornmeal, baking powder, anise seed, salt, and baking soda.

In a large bowl, with an electric mixer, beat the butter and ½ cup of the sugar on medium speed until fluffy, 3 to 4 minutes. Add the eggs, one at a time, and the vanilla. In three additions, alternate adding the flour mixture and the sour cream, starting with the flour mixture. Add the batter to the prepared skillet and smooth the top. Fan the fruit slices on top of the batter, placing them in a decorative pattern if you wish. Sprinkle the top with the remaining tablespoon sugar.

Bake until the cake is golden in the spots where it peeks through the fruit and a toothpick inserted into the center comes out with moist crumbs attached, 40 to 45 minutes. Let cool slightly on a rack before slicing. (Make sure to wrap the handle in a towel for safety.)

This cake is best the day it's made, but you can store leftovers, well wrapped, at room temperature for up to 2 days.

BLACKBERRY-LAVENDER CLAFOUTIS

SERVES 8

1¼ cups whole milk

1 teaspoon dried lavender buds

⅓ cup plus 2 tablespoons granulated sugar

1 vanilla bean, split and seeds scraped

½ cup (2¼ ounces) all-purpose flour

½ cup heavy cream

2 large eggs plus 2 large egg yolks

1 teaspoon pure vanilla extract

Pinch of kosher salt

2 tablespoons unsalted butter

12 ounces (3 cups) fresh blackberries

Confectioners' sugar, for sprinkling

Clafoutis [kla-foo-TEE] is even more fun to eat than it is to say, if you can believe it. The texture is somewhere in between cake, custard, and crêpe, and pure magic. The berries get a nice roll-around in a little butter and sugar to soften them slightly and bring out their juices. Baked in the lavender-scented custard, their floral sweetness only intensifies. This beauty is best eaten warm, when the lightly caramelized edges are still a little crispy. Look for pretty, purple-hued lavender buds in the spice section of a well-stocked supermarket.

In a small saucepan, bring the milk and lavender to a boil over medium heat. Remove from the heat and let stand, covered, for at least an hour.

Preheat the oven to 450°F.

In a large bowl, blend ⅓ cup of the sugar and the vanilla bean seeds with your fingers. Whisk in the flour. Gradually whisk in the heavy cream until a smooth paste forms. Whisk in the eggs, egg yolks, vanilla extract, and salt. Set a fine-mesh sieve over the flour mixture. Strain the lavender milk mixture into the flour mixture and stir until smooth.

In a 10-inch ovenproof skillet (both stainless steel and cast-iron work well), melt the butter over medium-high heat. Add the remaining 2 tablespoons sugar and swirl the pan to combine. Cook until the mixture just begins to caramelize, 1 to 2 minutes. Decrease the heat to medium, add the blackberries, and gently stir to combine. Cook 1 minute more to warm the berries and coat them in the sauce. Remove from the heat and immediately add the milk mixture. Don't forget to scrape the vanilla bean seeds from the bottom of the bowl into the skillet.

Bake until the edges are puffed, the top is golden, and the center is set and no longer runny, 15 to 20 minutes. Let cool slightly, then sprinkle with confectioners' sugar and serve warm.

ACKNOWLEDGMENTS

Without the kindness, wisdom, and generosity of many wonderful people, this book would simply not exist. Those people will have a spot in my heart forever.

Liz Pearson, Melissa Pellegrino, Don Morris, Cary Midland Sheehan, and Susan Westmoreland took the time to make millions of scary red marks all over early drafts of my book proposal. Their insights and cheerleading helped me get this project off the ground.

I loved every second of my years sharing burners with the brilliant teams behind *Martha Stewart Living* and *Everyday Food* (RIP), *Fine Cooking*, and *Good Housekeeping*. So many people have learned to cook and eat better thanks to all of them. Myself included.

My agent Janis Donnaud told me when to have faith and when to stop being hysterical. And she always had my back. I know how lucky I am to have her as a coach and advocate.

Jenny Abramson, Erin Chapman, B Chatfield, Juliet Gorman, Allison Dewine Kociuruba, Amy Leo, Cathy Lo, Abby Simchak, Katie Stilo, Lauren Tempera, and Sarah Rosenthal made up my army of intrepid recipe testers. They challenged my methods, convinced me to make some nuts optional, and ate more dessert than they probably wanted to. Jessica Fox and Jessie Damuck deserve special gold stars. I want to bake them all a billion cakes.

Merritt Watts was editor, recipe tester, restaurant supply store, housing and activities coordinator, and buddy all in one. She and Brian Turner are great friends, lovely hosts, and excellent amateur prop stylists. Megan Hedgpeth and Jim Conmy's early contributions to the making of this book empowered me to keep going.

A million thanks to Erin Kunkel for these gorgeous images, to Ethel Brennan for her perfect props, and to Jason Schreiber for his food-styling magic. Together they made my (very brown) recipes pop.

The extraordinary, brilliant, and dedicated team at Ten Speed Press—Jenny Wapner, Emily Timberlake, Ashley Lima, Emma Campion, and crew—turned my golden syrup–stained notebook into a book I am truly proud of. I hope they are proud of the result, too.

Deborah Keefe, John Sedgewick, and the rest of the Keefe, Sedgewick, and Marsidi clan are my favorite taste testers. Now I'm taking requests.

Nirmala Goonewardene, Ananda Seneviratne, Janet Seneviratne, Mala Senaratne, Tissa Seneviratne, Kusum Ekenayake, Senaka Ekenayake, Cuda Wijeyratne, Chandrika Magalle, and Anomi Pethiyagoda Kangara drank tea with me while I pestered them with questions and begged for family photos. Thank you!

Thanks to my parents, Suneetha and Upali Seneviratne. Because of them, I have equal love for boxed brownie mix and homemade love cake. Their sense of humor, stories, and love fill the pages of this book. I would have nothing to write about without them.

My husband Augustine Sedgewick encourages me to be the best Sen I can be every day. His love and edits make me a better person and a better writer. Jackpot!

And of course, thank you to the dear readers of this book and Love, Cake. I'd love to share a cookie and a chat with each of you. I am so grateful for your support.

INDEX